The New Majority

The New Majority

Adult Learners in the University

Duncan D. Campbell

 The University of Alberta Press

First published by
The University of Alberta Press
Athabasca Hall
Edmonton, Alberta
Canada   T6G 2E8

Copyright © The University of Alberta Press 1984

ISBN 0-88864-045-5 paper
ISBN 0-88864-097-8 cloth

Canadian Cataloguing in Publication Data

  Campbell, Duncan D., 1919–
    The new majority

  Bibliography: p.
  ISBN 0-88864-045-5 paper
  ISBN 0-88864-097-8 cloth

  1. Continuing education — Canada. 2. Adult
  education — Canada. 3. Universities and colleges —
  Canada. I. Title.
  LC5254.C35   1984   374'.971   C84-091063-0

All rights reserved.
No part of this publication may be produced, stored in a retrieval system, or transmitted in any form or by any means, electronic, mechanical, photocopying, recording, or otherwise, without prior permission of the copyright owner.

Typesetting by Solaris Press, Inc., Rochester, Michigan

Printed by Hignell Printing Limited, Winnipeg, Manitoba, Canada

Institutions of society, like species of animals, adapt themselves not in anticipation of changes in the environment but in response to changes that have already occurred.

> Sir Eric Ashby, Master of Clare College, Cambridge, *Adapting Universities to a Technological Society*

Contents

Tables and Figures   ix
Preface   xi
1 **University Continuing Education: A Retrospect**   1
   The Development of University Continuing Education in Canada   5
   Part-time Students: The New Majority   12
2 **The Rhetoric of University Continuing Education**   25
3 **University Continuing Education Program**   43
   Part-time Courses for University Credit   44
   Professional and Paraprofessional Studies   48
   Liberal and General Studies   53
   Community Development   57
   Community Services   60
4 **The Design and Delivery of University Continuing Education**   64
   The Bases of Continuing Education Design   64
   Program Choice and Development   68
   Counselling the Adult Learner   73
   Instructional Technology   75
   Accreditation: The Continuing Education Unit   79
   Innovative Practices In Continuing Education   82
   Evaluating the Product   85

5 **Organization and Policies** 89
   Function: The Basis of Structure 90
   Structuring University Continuing Education 92
   External Relationships in University Continuing
      Education 99
   Finance and Accountability 102
   Staffing 105
   Marketing Continuing Education 108
   Research 111
   The Responsibility of Government 115
6 **University Continuing Education: The Prospect** 119
   Public Expectations of the University 120
   Strategies for Change 125
   Formulating Continuing Education Policy 128
   References Cited 135

Tables and Figures

Tables

1 Registrations in Continuing Education in Selected Public Education Institutions, 1972–73 and 1975–76   15
2 Numbers of Registrations and Participation Rates per 1,000 of Population in Part-time Credit and Formal Noncredit University Continuing Education Courses, by Province, 1975–76   16
3 Registrations in University Continuing Education by Program Category and by Province, 1975–76   17
4 Registration in University Noncredit Courses by Field of Study, 1975–76   19

Figures

1 Typical Formats of University Continuing Education Programs   67
2 Decision Points and Components of a Continuing Education Program   68
3 Functional Areas of Research and Development in Higher Education Management   114

Preface

Since World War II when, suddenly, the importance of universities became obvious to the nation, almost every facet of these institutions as partners in the higher education network has been analyzed in detail—except university continuing education.

Preoccupied with the expansion of its more traditional functions, universities seem scarcely to have noticed a significant change in the character of the student body. The traditional clientele of the university had long been youth aged 18 to 24 engaged in full-time study. But today, adult learners in part-time credit courses and in formal noncredit programs together outnumber the full-time student body. These adult learners are the new majority. In a society pushed and pulled by an ever-expanding technology, in which it is no longer feasible to accomplish the whole of one's education for life on the basis of "front end load," this new majority has become a conspicuous and likely permanent part of the universities' clientele.

This book is about the education of these adult learners. Its focus is not the activities which characterize contemporary "extension work." Rather, it is an analysis of the role of the university—as an element of the higher education network—in the provision of learning opportunities to adults. As such, its end purpose is to establish a matrix of guidelines within which individual institutions, each according to its own circumstances, can assess the policies and structures which it has provided for this function.

This study invites the interest of legislators who allocate fund support to universities (and whose ears are tuned to citizen concerns about higher education), of academics who are uncomfortably aware that the size of the conventional student body on which university funding is based may well decline, of citizens conscious of personal needs for refresher training and education arising mostly out of changes in their lives, and all of those many engaged in the function itself. While the setting of the work is Canada, much of the analysis is relevant as well to university and college institutions in the United States and the Commonwealth countries.

Published work on continuing education is disparate in its sources. Much other writing on the subject is fugitive and, generally, this scattered literature is not well known. Hence, this account makes generous reference to a wide array of books, official documents, articles and unpublished papers drawn from American, British and Canadian sources which will help the reader to enlarge his grasp of this expanding field.

In such a study as this, one is inevitably a debtor to many, among whom are colleagues whose helpful candor and questioning have shaped the work. Anne LeRougetel and Monica Jewell have been painstaking and expert in the preparation of the manuscript.

The author wishes to record his gratitude to the Canada Council, to Imperial Oil Limited and to the Department of Advanced Education, Government of Alberta, for fund support of this study, and to the Faculty of Extension, The University of Alberta, which gave its encouragement. This book has been published with the help of a grant from the Social Science Federation of Canada, using funds provided by the Social Science and Humanities Research Council of Canada.

To all of these, though none is in any way responsible for the views expressed, it is a pleasure to express grateful thanks.

Duncan D. Campbell

1 University Continuing Education
A Retrospect

Prior to World War II, universities in Canada occupied a quiet backwater — little understood artifacts standing at society's fringes. But since 1940, their potential to serve the country having become obvious and important, they have been the object of extensive study and review: how they should be funded, their research function, student access to them, their organization and governance and the role of students and staff. Indeed, few facets of university operation have not been thoroughly scanned — with an exception. What has largely escaped the attention of researchers is the expanded role of Canadian universities in public service, particularly in continuing education, which changes in technology reflected in society have made of likely permanent importance.

University public service is an extension of the institution to society at large in such a fashion as to bring its special competence to bear on issues and problems. It is manifested in four ways: criticism and advice by members of the academic community on technical problems and social issues; the presentation of cultural and other events; the preservation of the cultural heritage of the country for future generations in libraries, galleries and museums; and continuing education, the provision of specialized instruction to those other than its conventional clientele.

A number of factors have pressed the university to an expansion of its public service role (Corson 1968). Its resources of staff, buildings and equipment aside, the university affords a certain prestige, an agreeable ambiance within which problems can be tackled. It has acquired not a monopoly but a substantial pool of a particular kind of human talent capable of dealing with a variety of problems. The university stresses objectivity, the detached approach of those not habituated to one mode of thought. Through basic research, universities are committed to acquiring new understanding which becomes more important when human advancement, based on tinkering and improvisation on present knowledge, dwindles. But importantly, the university possesses values, civilizing values, of which the most important is freedom. Threaded through all of this is the judgment in some minds that, through participation in public service, the scholar can infuse his teaching and research with greater vividness, a heightened sense of reality, and be enabled to link his scholarship with the realities of contemporary practice in the world beyond the university's walls.

Yet there is a small core of academics to whom public service is irrelevant, a function inconsistent with the academy's fundamental responsibility of teaching youth and discovering new knowledge. In their view, it is the duty of the university not to proffer institutional services but to protect the integrity of the academy. To them, the conception of the university as an activist shaper of the larger society is anathema; separateness from society and freedom to set its own goals independent of society is essential to the optimum development of the institution whose prime function is the critical appraisal of society and the diagnosis of its ills. In consequence, the university must remain *irresponsible* in its relationship to society (Campbell, 1977a). Both this perspective of the university and another which stands in striking contrast, that of the university as an institution obliged by a radically changing society to serve the community, presume a strong commitment to the institution and a belief in its importance.

This conflict of belief lies behind the ambivalence of university leadership in its support of its public service role—which includes continuing education. In an address to his institution's constituents at convocation, a Canadian university president asserts that institutional priorities ought to be those perceived by university staff and not those proposed by other elements in society; but almost in the same breath, he urges that state universities in particular be sensitive to the needs of society as they are perceived by many sectors of the community and not just by academics. That ambivalence aside, a Carnegie report (1967) concludes that many universities are simply not governed in such a way as to permit them readily to determine and enunciate policy with respect to their public service role and calls for a modernization of university governance to reconsider all three of the functions, teaching, research and public service in which the typical university institution is today engaged. Such a process would have the salutary effect of focussing the entire academic community's thought on the function of public service which might lead to a reconception of university role which might better fit today's world. At the very least, it would underline a fact of more than institutional significance: that the university is inescapably linked to the viability of the contemporary knowledge-centered society.

What follows in this book is an analysis of a major element in university public service: continuing education. Its end purpose is to establish a matrix of guidelines which individual institutions, each according to its own circumstances, might use to assess the policies and structures which it has provided for that function. The reader will find first a review of the historical antecedents and development of university continuing education in Canada, an indication of its present extent and the characteristics of its clientele. A synthesis of the rhetoric of continuing education in Canada drawn from commission reports, the studies undertaken by individual universities, and researches conducted by agencies connected to the universities follows. Flowing out of this review is a sketch of the five chief segments of a university continuing education program — part-time courses for university credit, professional and para-professional studies, liberal and general studies, community development, and community services — and an assessment of the forces which shape each. Succeeding it and closely linked is an analysis of how programs of continuing education are conceived, developed and delivered. Examined next is the function itself, its reflection in structure, its significant external relationships, the role of government with respect to it, and its policies in these specifics: finance, staffing, marketing and research. The book concludes with an estimate of public expectations of universities in continuing education, a recapitulation of the key issues inherent in this field and, in the light of these, a synopsis of possible strategies for change in institutional conduct of the continuing education enterprise.

Adult education, the generic term, is ubiquitous, pervasive and quite possibly outranks motherhood, apple pie and the flag as a universal good (Cross 1978). To no other term in education is ascribed such a welter of meanings, some seemingly synonymous and often used interchangeably (Campbell 1977b). *Further education*, for example, as often used appears to define that broad range of educational experience following schooling directed toward the young. In United Kingdom usage, it refers rather more specifically to training intended to enable young learners to gain entry to the job market or to cope with job obsolescence. *Extramural studies* is a term favored by British universities for what in Canada would be termed continuing education—and which emphasizes its separateness from the institution. *Recurrent education* suggests the periodic return of adults to learning to enable them better to cope with social or vocational change. In more opulent societies, it suggests the setting aside by adults of periods in their lives dedicated to full-time study aimed at personal development. A relative newcomer to this lexicon is the European term *andragogy*, used to denote ". . . a relatively independent science concerning the education and training of adults" (Savicevic & others 1966, 771). *Education permanente* embraces a concept of education as a natural requirement throughout all of life and logically implies a restructuring of the whole of the educational system in such a way as to match learning experiences with growing maturity. Somewhat parallel, if less precisely defined, and perhaps best regarded as a kind of logo is the still-popular American term, *life-long learning*. *Extension education*, American in origin, connotes informal adult learning activities connected to agriculture, a spin-off from formal training in that field provided by U.S. land-grant university institutions. To these might be added such other terms as *cultural diffusion, adult basic education, community development*, and *community education*. None of these terms is used with precision. Each, however, has two elements in common: the maturity of the adult not simply in terms of age but in respect of his experience of life; and the act of learning.

The term favored by North American institutions of higher education, *continuing education*, is used to denote adult learning at an elevated level, including the advancement of professional or vocational competence, following initial formal training. It implies "a relationship between an educational agent and a learner in which the agent selects, arranges, and continuously directs a sequence of progressive tasks that provide systematic experiences to achieve learning for those whose participation in such activities is subsidiary and supplemental to a primary productive role in society" (Verner & others 1970, 6). In this book, the term continuing education is intended to include specific, continuous, formal educational activities which meet Verner's definition but not such heterogeneous activities as recitals, exhibitions, casual lectures or the operation of museums and galleries, valuable as these may be.

The Development of University Continuing Education in Canada

As with most of Canada's social institutions, the roots of university continuing education are to be found in Britain and in the United States.

In early nineteenth-century England, the social unrest which fostered the extension of suffrage, the growth of trade unions, the abolition of slavery and beginning concerns for human welfare raised other urgent questions. How was education to be provided to men and women who, as children, had been denied it by circumstances and the demands of the Industrial Revolution? How most productively for the whole of society was the power of the newly-organized workers to be exercised?

In the mid-nineteenth century, the Mechanics' Institutes provided an initial and popular vehicle for worker education. Originally intended as a device for the instruction in science of artisans by university men, these clubs soon came to serve a middle-class clientele. A product of discontent with this altered purpose and an instructional format of single lectures, Oxford's Ruskin College was established in 1854 for a body of adult workers. With London's Birkbeck College, it lent encouragement first to the emergence of a university extension movement and later to the Worker's Educational Association (WEA) under whose auspices university lectures could be presented.

The WEA was a thrust of the then struggling labor movement which realized that if labor's aims were to be achieved, both leadership and membership would require more and better education. Founded in 1903, it attracted to itself workers active in the trade unions and the new Cooperative Movement and, as well, churchmen and intellectuals sympathetic to their aims. The establishment of a national system of education for all children irrespective of their social background or ability and the creation of such other facilities as would enable workers to develop their intellectual powers, thus to improve the conditions of their class, were the WEA's aims. The WEA had a significant impact on university adult education. In 1907, prompted by the demands of student workers, a clerk in the Cooperative Wholesale Society, Albert Mansbridge, was invited to request from the universities not merely occasional lectures but systematic and sustained courses of study under university direction. Thus began a remarkably fruitful cooperation between the WEA and the universities reflected in the creation of tutorial classes which required of the student attendance at twenty-four successive sessions annually, the preparation of papers, and extensive reading. Among the addresses presented to a joint committee of workers and Oxford professors which established these tutorials is this eloquent and still pertinent plea from a wheelwright:

> What is the true function of a University? Is it to train the nation's best men, or to sell its gifts to the rich? Instead of recruiting her students from the widest possible area, she has restricted her area of selection to the fortunate few. They come to her not for intellectual training, but for veneering. Not only are workpeople deprived of the right of access to that which belongs to no class or caste, the accumulated knowledge and experience of the race, but Oxford herself misses her true mission, while the nation and the race lose the services of its best men. . . . I wish it to be remembered that workpeople could do far more for Oxford, than Oxford can do for the workpeople . . . if Oxford continues to stand apart from the workpeople, then she will ultimately be remembered, not for what she is but for what she has been (Mansbridge 1913, 194).

Thus, the special feature of university continuing education in Britain was a partnership with working-class citizens intended to ameliorate critical social and political problems. The product of democratic aspirations, university continuing education in Britain developed—and the point is worth noting—not as a spontaneous initiative from within the universities but as a somewhat reluctant response to citizen needs expressed beyond its walls. A notable achievement of this new extension movement was its direct support to the expansion of conventional university work through encouragement given to the establishment of new university colleges. Indeed, when Cambridge instituted its local lectures syndicate in 1873, there were only three other universities in England (Oxford, London and Durham) and four in a much less densely populated Scotland. Some three decades later, there were twice as many new centers of full-time university work as there had been which had, or were expectant of, full university status. Of these, more than half owed their development to the work of Oxford and Cambridge extension centers.

Time and circumstances have changed. But a landmark document of that era, the so-called *"1919 Report"* (*Design for Democracy*, 1956), prepared jointly by academics and workers, remains a most eloquent yet practical statement of university purpose in continuing education which deserves the careful attention of the contemporary reader.

The roots of the American educational system, the diversity and extent of which astonish the visitor to the United States, lie in the determination of the first settlers in Massachusetts to protect and extend the religious beliefs which had prompted them to chance that frontier. Four attitudes of politicians, educational theorists and the public are commonly held to have shaped the system. Education should be inspired by practical, felt needs. Education was not only a powerful and effective tool for the development of the country but for citizens, it was an avenue to power. Education was a responsibility of government which had the duty to sponsor and encourage it. Education ought to be readily available to all citizens— but yet be guided by public opinion. These beliefs, still operative, comprise the philosophical set which inspired university continuing education development in the United States.

In the latter half of the nineteenth century, the thrust of scientific advance with its consequent applications in technology spurred industrialization and transformed the settled East from a rural to an urban society. This period saw the expansion of state universities and the creation of school systems each infused with a clear sense of responsibility to society. As early as 1808, a Yale University professor had presented popular lectures to the public; Johns Hopkins University, almost from its beginnings in 1876, served the Baltimore community with external courses. But indisputably, it was the Morrill Act of 1862, creating land-grant colleges with a mandate to promote liberal and practical education and to encourage the study of agriculture and the mechanical arts, which was the critical step in the democratization of higher education and the genesis of contemporary university continuing education (Carey 1961).

Meanwhile, off the campus, two ideas were developing which were to stimulate the extension of the university. The first of these was the Lyceum, the conception of a Connecticut farmer who concluded that cooperative study by groups of neighbors would be mutually profitable. Over time, the idea of such study groups travelled to the south and midwest where it took the shape of a formal lecture circuit which, after the Civil War, became a commercial enterprise dedicated less to education than to net profit. The second and more significant idea was the Chautauqua which began as a rural-based summer school of two weeks, its purpose to combine mental stimulation with physical recreation. This, too, was transformed by entrepreneurs into a kind of educational circus. It persisted across rural America and was an occasional feature of rural life in Canada until the 1930s. The Lyceum and the Chautauqua, and to a lesser extent the example of Oxford and Cambridge in projecting themselves through external lectures, were a sharp stimulus to American universities. Urged on by a handful of American scholars, among them Herbert Baxter Adams of Johns Hopkins, the extension of the university within the United States to the public at large had become commonplace by 1890.

William Rainey Harper, the first President of the new University of Chicago, gave the extension of the university a new dimension. Fresh from his association with Chautauqua and now responsible for the design of that new institution, he incorporated university extension into it as one of its five major divisions. Previous attempts to transfer the concept of British extramural studies to the American scene had not been fully successful because of the failure to recognize the realities of the open social class structure of the United States. Equally important, the motivation to adult education in the United States was essentially economic whereas in Britain it had been political and ideological. Harper's accomplishment in the last decade of the nineteenth century was a university extension program directly suited to American needs of that time. It centered on university courses acceptable for credit lifted out of the regular curriculum and offered at times and places convenient to the public (Dunkel & Fay 1968; Gould 1961).

The transformation of towns into metropolitan areas, the influx of immigrants, the growth of industry and the technical requirements of American agriculture all spurred a reaching out by the university institution, exemplified at the turn of the century by the University of Wisconsin. Its President, Charles R. Van Hise, a vigorous exponent of university extension, weighing the opposition of his staff against support of forces off the campus including the State government and the merchants, proposed that the campus of his university should be the whole of the State. "The broadest ideal of service demands that the university, as the best-fitted instrument, shall take up the problems of carrying out knowledge to the people. . . . It is apparent that [this] work . . . is one of enormous magnitude and not inferior in importance or in opportunity to the functions of the university earlier recognized—those of instruction and research" (Van Hise 1915, 7–24). The Wisconsin experiment flourished and gave new vitality to the already broad development of university extension in the United States. Moreover, its example provided leadership to Western Canadian institutions, among them the fledgling universities of Saskatchewan and Alberta.

Social forces similar to those operative in the United States, and the British experience with adult education influenced the shape of university continuing education in Canada though their impact is not crisply defined.

Canadian adult education had its beginnings in the Mechanics' Institutes which had arrived with immigrants in the nineteenth century. But the environment in which the Institutes now found themselves was radically different. In a new country with limited political and industrial sophistication, they were adopted by educational and political leaders as a device to provide lectures by academics and professionals. Largely confined to what was then Upper and Lower Canada, they survived only until the end of the century; but for a few decades, they provided a vehicle through which universities might offer their wares to the public. The disappearance of the Mechanics' Institutes left clear the field of popular education. The idea of the Lyceum and the Chautauqua, developed in the United States with enthusiasm, success and ultimately profit, did not truly catch the interest of Canadians.

In 1889, Queen's University took the initiative in establishing extramural work and in 1892 its Principal convened a meeting for the purpose of exploring the means of extending university service to the people of Quebec and Ontario. Little seems to have resulted from it; the financial restrictions of government and the indifference of the universities effectively dampened any aspirations of the public for the extension of higher education.

The first vigorous thrust in the development of university continuing education to incorporate field work came from Western Canada. Only two years after its inception, Walter Charles Murray, the first President of the University of Saskatchewan, claimed this goal for his institution: "Its watchword is service . . . No form of that service is too mean or too exalted for the university. It is . . . fitting for the university . . . to place within the reach of [members of the public] opportunities for adding to their stores of knowledge and enjoyment . . . There should be ever present the consciousness that this is the University of the people, established by the people, and devoted by the people to the advancement of learning and the promotion of happiness and virtue" (Murray 1909, 11–12).

In neighboring Alberta at the same time, Henry Marshall Tory, fresh from the university establishment of the East, became the first President of The University of Alberta. Like Murray, a vigorous man with strongly held opinions, he brought with him the sophisticated notions of higher education of that day. But, as well, both were strongly influenced by the ambitious populist approach to public service of the University of Wisconsin typified by its motto, "Our campus the state." Politically apt, thoroughly aware of what the social environment demanded of his institution, conscious that a new university had to win and hold public confidence, Tory acknowledged of Alberta's small and scattered population that "many of them will never see the place, much less have an opportunity of attending, or having their children attend, its classes. Yet we want the citizens of the province to feel that the university belongs to them, that it exists to serve them. The time may come when the existence of a university will depend upon the public's assurance that its thinking and research are of vital importance to the community. The job of the extension department is to find out from the people what the university can do for them beyond the classroom and the laboratory" (Corbett 1954, 100–1). Through lectures and debates, through the magic lantern, through the enchantment of moving pictures, by means of rural conferences and demonstrations of agricultural techniques in which railway coaches served as travelling classrooms, and through its agricultural bulletins, the universities in these adjoining provinces reached into most prairie homes.*

There were two other developments in the emergence of university continuing education in Canada shortly after the turn of the century. The first was the importation of the Workers' Educational Association (WEA) at the conclusion of World War I. (A quite remarkable if short-lived experiment in the extension of the university had been the creation of a "Khaki College" in Britain for Canadian troops on leave from the trenches). As in England, the WEA was aimed at fostering and meeting the demand for education at the university level from working men. Encouraged by the University of Toronto and Queen's University, the WEA was able to sustain itself until World War II though it did not flourish and had only minimal impact on university continuing education. The second development — one which gave Canada international prominence in adult education — was the support given by St. Francis Xavier University in the two decades after World War I to an enterprise, subsequently labeled the Antigonish Movement. Led by Dr. James Tompkins and Dr. M.M. Coady, the Movement helped impoverished fishermen of the Maritime Provinces to restructure their economic circumstances. Working directly with the fishermen, in a very real sense as educational missionaries, and

---

*The most widely read technical book in the whole of Alberta at that time, a runaway best-seller, was Bulletin No. 10, 1925, *Binder and Knotter Troubles*, J. MacGregor Smith, published by the University of Alberta's Faculty of Agriculture and regularly reprinted over two decades.

emphasizing the application of cooperative principles, these university men enabled the people of this depressed area to establish better lives for themselves through education.

But continuing education as a university function did not begin to develop in any extensive fashion in Canada until the end of World War II. In the United States, the growth and broad acceptance of university extension was illustrated by the formation in 1915 of the National University Extension Association; its sister organization, the Canadian Association of Directors of Extension and Summer School, did not emerge until the 1950s.

As Houle notes in his excellent little essay (1952), until 1900 the efforts of universities in Great Britain, Canada and the United States in continuing education were roughly parallel. Since then, each has matured in its own way. The British institutions have concerned themselves in the main with teaching and with emphasis on formal education incorporating traditional university standards. American universities, by contrast, have provided an extraordinarily wide range of services in addition to teaching but, it is alleged, with these tendencies: a triviality of program; an emphasis on public relations; a concentration on profits; and an attempt at monopoly. A development unique to the United States is its extraordinarily successful agricultural extension enterprise, cooperative extension, in which the university is a partner with government. Canadian institutions have blended teaching and other services; but in recent years, they have been much more influenced by the American approaches than by those of the British. In Canadian practice, the errors appear to be principally those of omission. Its universities have come late to an appreciation of the opportunities to serve the public — and themselves — through continuing education. Although there is satisfaction in recollecting the internationally recognized accomplishments of the Antigonish Movement, the creation of the prestigious Couchiching Conference and the establishment of the Banff Centre for Continuing Education, Canadian universities, until midway in this century, have shown reluctance to assume the education of adults as a serious responsibility.

Part-time Students: The New Majority

A variety of forces spur the growth of continuing education of which the most ubiquitous is the pace of technological advance, its effect on society dramatically illustrated today by the silicon chip. As Ricardo, the eighteenth-century British economic theorist observed, while it may be difficult to deal with technological change, it is disastrous to ignore it. Clearly, its most obvious consequence today is that it is no longer feasible to acquire the whole of one's education on the basis of "front-end load."

The role of women in the workplace has shifted markedly. Technology and child-care facilities permit their involvement in the labor force (of which they now comprise over half) while economic pressures on families combined with the rising expectations of women of productive lives of their own will support the trend. Leisure time has become more than simply time off from work: North Americans are choosing it over longer working hours and higher incomes and doubtless they will invest part of it in education. The range of learning interests of adults has expanded. Adult learners have adopted a format of non-sequential or recurring education to an extent quite unpredictable even a decade ago. It is a commonplace today for education to be interrupted for periods of work or travel or reflection. Education and training connected to those interests are not necessarily confined to a single source. Would-be learners tend to move across educational sectors, from provider to provider as, for example, from college to university to technical school to industry-provided in-service training services to museum recreation classes. Today's students seek a mix of educational experience to maximize "self-actualization." Substantial proportions of the already well-educated engage in continuing education to facilitate voluntary or required mid-career change. And such demographic and social features as these will continue to generate needs in continuing education: the increase in life-expectancy and the decline in work–life expectancy; personal crises which result from family difficulties, divorce and the problems of the increasingly frenetic middle years of adult life; and boredom or frustration in employment which engender job alienation.

These are indisputably significant signals from society to educators. But in North America, educational policy has generally focussed upon the *core*; in consequence, public information agencies, including government statistics agencies, and policy makers have tended to give precedence to the gathering of information about core activities (Moss 1971). This, manifestly, has political implications for the body of adult learners, since decisions are unlikely to be taken about a body of students and their educational interests which in statistically descriptive terms are not well documented.

That is the dilemma of Canadian adult education. In the United Kingdom, data descriptive of the continuing education phenomenon is reported by the Department of Education and Science in *Statistics of Education (England and Wales), Further Education*, Volume 3. These are fleshed out by additional reports from Wales, Scotland and Northern Ireland and the whole is periodically supplemented by reports such as *Adult Education: A Plan for Development* (1973). In the United States, detailed information based on triennial surveys is gathered by the National Center for Educational Statistics, Department of Education and periodically interpreted in a document, *Condition of Education*. A sharp shift in U.S. attitude towards adult learning is underlined by the recent creation of a National Commission on Non-Traditional Study and by the fresh interest of the major foundations in learning experiences falling outside of the traditional mode. Incomprehensibly, Statistics Canada does not now gather data about the education of adults.

What can be documented, however, is that in 1974–75, adult learners in credit and formal noncredit courses in Canada became the new majority within the university's clientele. While full-time university registration, graduate and undergraduate was 347,000, the number of students engaged in part-time credit courses was 179,000 and those involved in formal noncredit studies numbered 214,000, a total of 384,000. Some of the part-time credit students, to be sure, were simply regular students undertaking make-up or supplemental studies. But the bulk of them were adults continuing their education.

Participation in university continuing education in Canada would most appropriately be examined could it first be viewed as an element of the whole fabric of adult education provision by a host of agencies. No such data are available. But the statistics in Table 1 which indicate the extent of public involvement in continuing education offered by the conventional educational institutions alone are instructive. As is evident, the universities' share of the "market" is 30 percent. The credit work of each of the four types of institutions has grown slowly while their noncredit work has more than doubled. The shares in the market attributed to each of the four appear to be shifting in favor of the community colleges.

TABLE 1
Registrations in Continuing Education in Selected Public Education Institutions, 1972–73 to 1975–76

	SCHOOL BOARDS, DEPARTMENTS OF EDUCATION		DEPARTMENT OF EDUCATION CORRESPONDENCE COURSES		COMMUNITY COLLEGES		UNIVERSITIES		TOTAL
	Part-time credit	Noncredit	Part-time credit	Noncredit	Part-time credit	Noncredit	Part-time credit	Noncredit	
1972–73	268,101	599,125	97,813	5,524	125,335	166,759	373,452	195,584	1,831,693
1973–74	256,252	616,426	101,082	6,801	135,162	193,783	373,485	258,616	1,941,607
1974–75	241,629	686,097	107,473	10,561	173,464	294,490	401,483	278,762	2,193,959
1975–76	232,888	835,873	124,610	14,345	178,675	377,542	463,604	284,180	2,511,718

Source: Statistics Canada, *Continuing Education: Participation in Programs of Educational Institutions, 1975–76*, Catalogue 81-253 (Ottawa, November 1977).

TABLE 2
Numbers of Registrations and Participation Rates* per 1,000 of Population in Part-time Credit and Formal Noncredit University Continuing Education Courses, by Province, 1975–76

	Registration – Part-time Credit Number	Part-time Credit Participation Rate	Registrations – Formal Noncredit Number	Formal Noncredit Participation Rate	Total Registrations Number	Participation Rate
Newfoundland	8,777	17.8	3,289	8.0	12,066	25.7
Prince Edward Island	2,679	28.9	102	1.1	2,781	29.9
Nova Scotia	15,069	23.6	7,886	11.5	22,955	35.1
New Brunswick	16,530	23.1	5,791	10.5	22,321	33.5
Quebec	138,655	25.2	50,863	9.5	189,518	34.6
Ontario	177,434	25.1	93,925	13.2	271,359	38.3
Manitoba	25,511	27.7	12,204	14.0	37,715	41.7
Saskatchewan	17,554	22.7	18,653	23.8	36,207	46.5
Alberta	33,246	18.1	47,212	31.6	80,458	49.6
British Columbia	28,149	10.3	44,255	20.3	72,404	30.6
Canada	463,604	22.7	284,180	14.5	747,784	37.1

*Within the population fifteen years of age and over who are not in full-time attendance at an educational institution.

Source: Statistics Canada, Continuing Education: Universities, 1975–76, Catalogue 81–225 (Ottawa, August 1977).

TABLE 3
Registrations in University Continuing Education by Program Category and by Province, 1975–76

	Canada	Newfound-land	Prince Edward Island	Nova Scotia	New Brunswick	Quebec	Ontario	Manitoba	Saskat-chewan	Alberta	British Columbia
PART-TIME CREDIT											
Part-time Credit (Regular Session and Summer Session)	463,604	8,777	2,679	15,069	16,530	138,655	177,434	25,511	17,554	33,246	28,149
FORMAL NONCREDIT											
Professional Development:											
Extension Diploma	45,359	992	8	460	465	16,633	18,107	1,467	301	4,038	2,888
Association Diploma	45,369	226	40	1,137	213	7,588	24,640	—	140	5,406	5,979
No Diploma	106,076	627	23	3,756	1,203	17,647	29,702	6,554	10,405	19,179	16,980
General Interest	87,376	1,444	31	2,533	3,190	8,955	21,476	4,183	7,807	18,589	18,408
Sub-total	284,180	3,289	102	7,886	5,791	50,863	93,925	12,204	18,653	47,212	44,255
Total	747,784	12,066	2,781	22,955	22,321	189,518	271,359	37,715	36,207	80,458	72,404

Source: Statistics Canada, *Continuing Education: Universities, 1975–76*, Catalogue 81–225 (Ottawa, August 1977).

Table 2 shows the extent of participation of Canadians in university continuing education and the *proportions* of adult learners engaged in its two principal formats: part-time credit and formal noncredit work.

What the data in Table 2 indicates is that public participation in 1975-76 stood at 37 percent (a figure 20 percent larger than 5 years earlier), that participation and a preference of adult learners for formal noncredit work tends to grow steadily as one moves from the older settled parts of the country to the newer regions. Between the populous central provinces and those in the west, that contrast is extreme.

Table 3 sets out the broad categories of continuing education programs in which students choose to register.

About two-thirds of all university continuing education students in Canada were registered in part-time credit work (on a roughly equal basis between the regular session and the summer session). Of those engaged in formal noncredit courses, about one-third were enrolled in diploma programs such as that of the Society of Industrial Accountants, the Certified General Accountants (which are professional qualifications), and the Institute of Canadian Bankers. The degree of interest in formal noncredit continuing education for professional development is much higher in the industrialized central provinces than elsewhere in Canada.

Table 4 indicates the specific subject fields in which students in university noncredit courses are engaged. Clearly, business management studies and those in the humanities and social sciences dominate student interest and together comprise over one-half of total registrations. Course work in the health sciences and in the fine and applied arts follow and make up 15 percent and 10 percent of total registrations respectively. The parallel with the United States experience is close. There, registrations reported by colleges and universities in noncredit continuing education followed this pattern of preference: business and management; fine and applied arts; health professions; physical education and avocational instruction; home economics; education; and interdisciplinary studies (NCES 1979-80).

Little is known of the subject preferences of students taking credit courses on a part-time basis. However, a 1972 Canadian study (Stager & Thomas) suggests that such registrations tend to be concentrated in arts and science programs since, at many universities,

TABLE 4
Registration in University Noncredit Courses by Field of Study, 1975–76

Business Management	66,171
Social Sciences	45,274
Health Sciences	41,201
Humanities	36,829
Fine and Applied Arts	28,229
Education	14,626
Mathematics and Computer Science	13,896
Primary Industries	10,908
Household Sciences	5,809
Natural Sciences	5,391
Engineering and Applied Sciences	5,051
Trade or Technical	3,222
Transportation and Communication	846
Special Programs for the Handicapped	47
Unclassified	6,080
Total	284,180

Source: Statistics Canada, Continuing Education: Universities, 1975–78, Catalogue 81-225 (Ottawa, August, 1977).

only courses in these areas are offered on a part-time basis and because the largest single group of students (though a declining number) are school teachers.

Figures alone conceal the human focus of these data: the adult who aspires to learn often under difficulty. It is the 29 year-old man with a wife and a new baby, who, at last perceiving that accounting is his niche, plods on over as many as eight years towards accreditation in that field. It is an ambitious senior school teacher who has set his mind on a school superintendency and seeks to advance his credentials. It is a member of a farmers' union with a vision of what might be in agriculture who undertakes to grapple with economics in preparation for a leadership role. It is a restless 43 year-old wife and mother who gains relief from household demands through the study of ceramics or comparative literature or who takes refresher courses in nursing techniques in anticipation of her re-entry into nursing. It is an engineering graduate, success having placed him in managerial ranks, who is confronted with human problems for which his earlier professional training has not prepared him. It is a new Canadian for whom more rewarding employment or access to formal post-secondary education requires that he upgrade his skill in English as a second language.*

Several current U.S. studies offer a profile of adult learners in that country (College Board 1980; Carp, Peterson & Roelfs 1974; National Center for Educational Statistics, periodic reports).** The first of these records that one-half of all adults—males and females equally—are engaged in some form of learning. Half of those are between the ages of 25–39. Nearly one-third have a four-year college or graduate or professional education. About a quarter have incomes in excess of $25,000. Over one-half are professional or technical people or managers, proprietors or officials. Over eighty percent are engaged in their continuing education because of life changes. Of those life changes, 56 percent are connected to career, 16 percent to family, and 13 percent to leisure. Twenty-seven percent of learners study on their own, 17 percent in employer-sponsored education/training, 15 percent at four-year universities/colleges, and four percent with professional associations. Indisputably, this is an extraordinary contemporary phenomenon.

Other supplemental facets of current American experiences of university continuing education in noncredit courses is reported by the N.C.E.S. in its 1979–80 survey. In the U.S.A., noncredit adult education activities were offered by all universities and 77 percent of all colleges and universities, a figure double that of ten years earlier. About 80 percent of public universities reported a centralized adult education unit (typically, an office for continuing education); yet the number of academic departments—particularly in business, nursing, education and music—which were engaged in noncredit continuing education activities increased by 50 percent from 1976 to 1978.

---

*Beyond the scope of this analysis of university continuing education but of considerable collateral interest is a comprehensive 1980 study, *Americans in Transition: Life Changes as Reasons for Adult Learning* conducted by the College Entrance Examination Board. It confirms that most adult decisions to seek educational renewal are clearly and directly related to significant changes—transitions—in their lives: those which affect careers, family situations, health, religion, or leisure opportunities. What emerges from the study is a pattern of serious learner intent and defined purpose. That not only permits responsive adult educational curriculum development but also invites a review by educational institutions of their responsibility to facilitate these transitions in adult lives through education.

**For a somewhat parallel study of adult learners in Ontario, see Ignacy Waniewicz, *"Demand for Part-time Learning in Ontario,"* O.I.S.E., 1976.

Registrations in colleges and universities for noncredit continuing activities increased by 15 percent from 1976-77 to 1977-78. Mandatory or optional professional education is stimulated variously by new occupational licensing requirements, by professional societies, by new problems or new laws. In the university sector, 39 percent of the adult education programs lay in continuing professional education. The breadth and intensity of that involvement is suggested by these figures: medicine (95 percent), nursing (90 percent), accounting (57 percent), engineering (48 percent), education (38 percent).

The Continuing Education Unit (CEU), almost unused in Canada, is a nationally recognized device in the USA for measuring and recording participation in a continuing education program that does not carry credit towards a degree but does meet established criteria. By 1977-78, the number of public universities using the CEU had increased to well over 80 percent.

Twenty-seven percent of public university institutions had public financial support; 75 percent of programs were self-supporting, 23 percent offered special student counselling, and 21 percent recorded credits which were subsequently converted into Full Time Equivalents (FTE).

What can be inferred from this assembly of data?

A prior question is the character of the data to which obvious caveats are attached. That from the United States, it must be conceded, reflects the different social order in that country and its different system of higher education. Because there is no agreement among Canadian institutions on the definition to be assigned to the terms used in the collection and compiling of data in continuing education, because of the heterogenous nature of the clientele served, because of the differences in the character of the continuing education "product," one speculates that, to some degree, such Canadian data as exists may be "soft." Nor are they as current as might be wished.

Yet, taken together, the data would seem to suggest directions in education which warrant the attention of all connected to the Canadian university system. The first is the rapid growth of university continuing education and, in contrast, the projected dwindling in size of the 18-24 age group which comprises the great bulk of full-time enrollees in university. By 1996, this group in Canada is expected to be 23 percent smaller than it was in 1982. On the continuing education side, meanwhile, part-time participation in university credit work has increased over the decade by 20 percent from 2.6 percent of the 20–30 age group to 3.1 percent in 1980. A growth of 40 percent in that age group between 1980 and 1996 is not unlikely. The message in short is this: if universities are to avoid being faced with enrollment declines from the mid-80s into the 90s, with all of the unhappy consequences which seem certain to follow, they must look to enlarging public participation in their resources. In order for universities to maintain their FTE enrollment during this period would require that every percentage-point shortfall in full-time participation be made up by a 3 percent increase in part-time participation in credit courses (Warren Clark 1982).*

What attention ought universities to pay to alternatives to conventional credit courses? Part of the answer lies in the exploding nature of technology and its impact of Canadian society. Expert and lay commentators agree that the introduction of micro-electronic or "chip" technology — to cite only one thrust in technology — will usher in a social revolution parallel in scope to that brought about by the Industrial Revolution (Zureik 1982). Present estimates of the proportion of the Canadian labor force likely to be engaged in the information business vary from between 30 to 40 percent. By 1985, it is anticipated that the information field will be Canada's largest employer and rank sixth in terms of sales revenue. This makes obvious not only the requirement of training of workers who will forward this revolution — and, of course, others — but of providing for the re-training on a continuing basis of those already so employed. Yet, it would seem unrealistic to assume that the latter, already with a substantial educational achievement, with considerable practical experience, and with the maturity that comes with shouldered responsibilities, would necessarily accept the instructional regimen employed to teach youth.

Together, the dwindling of the conventional student body and the seemingly inevitable increase in the body of part-time learners raise important questions to which universities must respond.

---

*A current report of the U.S. Census Bureau, *Current Population Reports, Series P-20*, No. 360, "School Enrolment — Social and Economic Characteristics of Students: October 1979," suggests a similar pattern.

It should be added, however, that as a consequence of the current depression and the scarcity of jobs, university enrollment has in fact risen recently. It seems likely that this unanticipated event is no more than a short-term aberration and that the earlier projected trend will develop.

Other avenues need to be explored: the determination of who the adult learners are who might be served by the university and their instructional needs; devising instructional modules which meet their requirements in terms of both content and methodology; infusing flexibility into the scheduling, the location, the length of courses.

A second part of the answer is suggested by the data above which indicate that the most likely participants in continuing education are those whose educational achievements (and income) are already the highest in society—which is precisely how one would describe the body of university alumni. This prompts the question: How important, how politic is it for the university to make a determined effort to provide for the continuing education of its own? The question is pertinent to institutions of higher education since they are by no means alone on the education frontier of the twenty-first century. According to a report by Cross (1981), in 1980, A.T. & T. spent four and a half times as much on the education of its employees as the Massachusetts Institute of Technology spent on the education of its students. The American Management Association, with an annual budget of $50 million, uses 7,500 lecturers and discussion leaders to conduct 2,000 formal education programs each year, and argues that it and other non-collegiate organizations ought to enter into competition with schools of business in graduate programs. Moreover, Cross argues, *degrees* are not essential for job mobility; it is only essential that *learning* be recognized by employers and potential employers. Employers can recognize any learning they consider relevant; and, clearly, those programs sponsored by employers themselves or by professional associations are highly relevant to workers' careers. Indeed, to the average adult, there is probably nothing more material to upward job mobility as noncredit, employer-managed programs of continuing education. This is reason to speculate that the university which neglects the continuing education of its graduates will have cause to regret it.

The roots of Canadian university continuing education are to be found in Britain and the United States. University attitudes towards public service—of which university continuing education is an element— are mixed, reflecting an ambivalence of opinion as to the role of the university, now pushed and pulled by changing technology with its manifold influences on society. This continuing education phenomenon is world-wide. Emerging internationally is a new philosophy of post-secondary education which incorporates the idea of "the learning society."

While university continuing education is well documented in other countries and particularly in the United States, little about the function in Canada is recorded in precise terms. Yet it seems apparent that university continuing education has become a vital component of education which universities cannot afford to ignore. Moreover, while public involvement in continuing education grows apace, the universities conventional student body is predicted to decline bringing in its train awkward and debilitating readjustments to those institutions. If the university is most productively to engage in new approaches to the education of what has become the bulk of its clientele, its policy makers need to inform themselves as to who these adult learners are, their learning interests and the real and perceived barriers to their participation in the life of the university.

At other times in their history, especially during and immediately after World War II, the academic community has met a like call without hesitation. Today's challenge is the needs of part-time learners, the new — and likely permanent — majority in higher education.

2   The Rhetoric of University Continuing Education

Canadian universities and agencies related to them have spent little time examining their engagement in continuing education. Nor are such principles as have emerged from their reviews necessarily reflected in continuing education provision on the campus. Yet it would seem useful to review something of the rhetoric of university continuing education as a backdrop against which subsequently to analyze the chief elements of its practice: program content, program design and delivery; and the structure and policies of the function. Commission reports, the studies undertaken by individual universities and researches by agencies connected to universities comprise the bulk of the analyses undertaken.

In commission studies conducted in every region of Canada in the last dozen years, the heightened visibility of continuing education is abundantly evident. Typifying their common tone are such extracts as these:

> . . . because knowledge and technology have expanded so much in the past decade and because life is becoming more complex socially, politically, economically and morally, education

must be thought of as a lifelong process (Newfoundland & Labrador 1968, 90).

. . . opportunities to pursue the goals of education should be available to all people at any time during their lives when need and desire for these opportunities arise (Nova Scotia 1974).

. . . continuing education is a transforming concept whose time has come and whose bracing impact will be felt (Ontario 1972, 22).

. . . we hold no other belief more strongly than that life-long education must be accepted, encouraged and fully supported (Manitoba 1973).

. . . continuing education [should] become a public service as extensive and widespread as traditional school education and even more diversified . . . [to] help the individual to make the best possible use of his . . . leisure time . . . self improvement or occupational retraining . . . but also for informing and developing the citizen (Quebec 1965, 326).

. . . the expansion of opportunities for further education — usually referred to as adult or continuing education — and the acceptance of public responsibility for their provision are urgent as was the establishment of the provision of elementary education almost a century ago (Alberta 1972, 59).

Nor are such sentiments confined to Canadian borders; they are replicated in parallel U.S. and British studies and internationally in a UNESCO document which concludes that "life-long education is the master concept for educational policies in the years to come for both developed and under-developed countries" (Faure 1972, 182).

These judgments are those of both professional educators and the well informed laymen who comprise these commissions. Lofty and even eloquent as are these statements, they have not been effective spurs to action. Nor would it seem that they are significantly reflected in university priorities. Interestingly, their perceived importance may vary widely depending on the institutional level consulted: a current American study demonstrates that "public service" (which includes continuing education) ranks third in importance among twenty institutional goals by the trustees of public universities, eighth by faculty and fourteenth by administrators (National Center for Higher Education Management Systems 1978).

Certain Canadian universities have themselves examined institutional purposes in continuing education.

In the force and conviction which infuse them, presidential statements from the western institutions dominate. For example, Henry Marshall Tory, the founding president of the University of Alberta acknowledged to its first convocation that

> the modern state university has sprung from a demand on the part of the people themselves for intellectual recognition, a recognition which only a century ago was denied them . . . The people demand that knowledge shall not be the concern of scholars alone. The uplifting of the whole people shall be its final goal . . . I consider that the extension of the activities of the university on such lines as will make its benefits reach directly or indirectly the mass of the people, carrying its ideals of refinement and culture into their homes and its latent spiritual and moral power into their minds and hearts, is a work second to none (Corbett 1954, 100–01).

Less evangelical in tone is a Dalhousie University report which concedes that "it is important to the University's own sense of direction and to its rightful status in the community that it be recognized and accepted as an institution existing primarily to provide, in its teaching function, opportunities at the postsecondary level for all who have the ability and desire to pursue academic study . . . [Dalhousie's] future growth and contribution to society will depend materially on how well it meets the needs of the 'new' students: the adults who are returning for further study; those who are turning for the first time to the University; and the professional graduates who recognize a need for assistance in keeping abreast of the latest knowledge and skills in their respective fields" (Dalhousie University 1976, 19).

Rather more pragmatically, the University of Western Ontario speculates that "Continuing Education programs, while providing important service to an increasingly large constituency, can allow the University to make full use of its resources even though the pool of traditional applicants to [the] University may shrink, will enhance the public image of the University, and will provide the opportunity to faculty to use their skills in diverse and innovative ways" (University of Western Ontario 1976, 1).

The most forceful expression of the university's role in continuing education is that of the President of the University of Lethbridge to the 1983 Macdonald Commission.

- Striking technological innovation may give rise to massive job dislocation and thus the need for unprecedented retraining; Canadian universities have an immediate role to play.
- Faculties of continuing education should replace the concept of learning as leisure with the concept of learning as accredited, certified, intellectual achievement.
- Universities should enlarge their commitment to interdisciplinary studies in all areas.
- Since the new economic order may abound with global implications, universities should adapt their curricula to global application.

Acknowledging a potential change in its future clientele, Trent University accepts that "society now regards learning to be more of a continuing process rather than a prelude to adult and professional life, and requires the alternative of a more fragmented approach to academic credits and flexibility to meet a wider range of educational needs" (Trent University 1974, 3).

A contrasting negative view of the University of Toronto (1970, 9) is that the very term "extension student" carries derogatory, apologetic, resentful, messianic and demarcatory overtones. The time is ripe, its report argues, not only to question the distinction between students thought to be fully in the university and those taken to be only half in, but also to make choices between activities proper to a university and those merely to be tolerated through inertia or misguided notions of public relations. The Toronto report concludes that the Extension Division having served the university and community well "should now be closed down."

But characteristically, throughout the range of such university reports is acknowledgment that the university can and should serve an adult constituency, that such service is mutually beneficial, that the prudent university ought to meet new educational demands spawned by a changing society and that adult learners ought to be serviced in a fashion consistent with their needs as adults.

But the same reports offer little evidence of study of what adult learning needs are or what they might be in the future though there is occasional recognition that continuing education programs ought not to be merely the product of estimates, guesses and hunches. A University of Lethbridge report predicts the gradual phasing out of the often arbitrary line which now divides formal schooling and continuing education (Selman & Sheats 1968, 37) while The University of Alberta (1974), noting anomalies between credit and noncredit work, proposes that the university should explore a wider variety of means through which the citizen can acquire a university education and should invest greater imagination in the delivery of continuing education programs to nonurban areas. Trent University (1974, 13), similarly, acknowledges the typical isolation of part-time students, the moral obligation to provide academically credible programs which serve the changing requirements of part-time students, noting prudently that "unless Trent reaches out and into our neighboring communities, other universities will move in to fill the void."

Of what comprises "university level" in programs, there is little discussion in university reports although certain guidelines were proposed to the University of Lethbridge:
- programs will be at an appropriate intellectual level in relation to university standards
- programs will reflect the university's standards of objectivity and analysis
- efforts will be made to offer programs which are experimental in terms of subject matter, methods and materials
- emphasis will be placed on interdisciplinary programs (Selman & Sheats 1968, 10–11).

With respect to the last of these, and as the University of Alberta acknowledges, though problems which our society faces are seldom encompassed by a single academic discipline, the growth of interdisciplinary programs is slow (Gunning 1975).

Until a decade ago, the universities' role in the training of professionals was primarily that of providing the basic initial training necessary to practice. This was satisfactory enough as long as the body of knowledge and skills required remained unchanged. But not only has the accumulation of new knowledge and new techniques accelerated, there have also been extraordinary changes in the social and political milieu in which professions are practiced. Though the environment has changed, Dalhousie University (1976) assigns the whole responsibility at that institution for continuing professional education solely to the professional faculties, which is generally what most Canadian universities have done.

A University of Lethbridge report observes that the continuing education functions funnels back into academic life benefits of considerable importance, among them the provision of opportunities for experimental classes, new approaches to subject-matter, and interdisciplinary courses, any of which may lead to modification of traditional campus courses and to educational innovations (Selman & Sheats 1968). By way of illustration, university continuing education efforts in Alberta and British Columbia, led not only to the establishment of university departments in drama, painting and music but also gave impetus to the development of community colleges and the University of Lethbridge.

What prompted Dalhousie University (1976) to examine its continuing education function were the practical issues concerned with its organization and administration: the extent of institutional responsibility for it; its publicity and coordination; community involvement in it; public accessibility to university programs; and the development and delivery of new programs.

Specific organizational issues are discussed in several of the university reports. The University of Lethbridge noting the not untypical isolation of the continuing education head recommends that he report directly to the president, that policies relevant to the continuing education function be subject to review by the academic Senate, that the *education* element of the function be clarified, and that the institutional commitment to continuing education be made plain (Selman & Sheats 1968).

McMaster University (1976) specifies three alternative models of organization of the continuing education function: a separate faculty or division of the university which assumes responsibility for all part-time study; a division which buys instruction from faculty members or from others outside the university on an overload basis; the acceptance of responsibility by individual faculties for all students, credit and noncredit alike, their registration, counselling, etc. In that institution's judgment, the concern for standards, programming and counselling can be best met by integrating the part-time and full-time programs which implies that all part-time students are in every way to be treated as full-time students. Similarly, Dalhousie argues that the primary responsibility for continuing education there be borne by each academic unit as an integral part of its commitment (Dalhousie University 1976). The University of Lethbridge, on the other hand, concludes that it is desirable that the administration of all continuing education activities, both credit and noncredit, be centralized in a separate division or faculty to ensure specialization of staff function, efficiency of administration, coordination of the demand upon the teaching and other resources of the institution, the articulation of interdisciplinary programs, and the consistent application of institutional policy (Selman & Sheats 1968). So, too, and for similar reasons, does the University of Victoria (1972) and the University of Western Ontario (1976). York University through its Atkinson College and the University of Toronto through its Woodsworth College on the other hand have established agencies exclusively to serve part-time students taking credit courses.

Almost invariably in Canadian universities, the participation of academic staff members in the institutions' programs of continuing education is voluntary and is encouraged by the payment of honoraria at a rate approaching that of consulting fees. This supplementary income, its justification and the implications of it is explored in a McGill report (McGill University 1966). But typically, such teaching is deemed not to fall within the range of the regular duties of the academic staff. Listed among the "Supplementary Professional Activities" itemized by the University of Alberta in a Board-Staff agreement are "teaching in the Summer Session, Spring Session, off-campus Evening Credit courses, Extension programs, etc." (University of Alberta 1977, 35). A University of Lethbridge report in contrast recommends that continuing education teaching be included within the range of expected staff duties (Selman & Sheats 1968, 22).

Clearly, and not surprisingly, there is little agreement on how the continuing education function is best organized. But what can be inferred from these reports is that success in serving the continuing education needs of the community will not be achieved by presidential fiat and the vitally necessary cooperation is conditional on an acceptance by the institution of responsibility for adult part-time learners. Nor, according to a New York University (1962) report, is a continuing education advisory and planning board the answer: these have hampered too many extension services to the verge of inanition.

The last decade has seen extraordinary growth not only in public participation in continuing education but in the proliferation of agencies which undertake its provision. Notable among these, an innovation principally of the last two decades in Canada, are the community colleges. No longer is the university the sole provider of learning opportunities to adults; today, indeed, it finds itself inevitably drawn into relationships with many other agencies and institutions.

Dalhousie University (1976) appropriately notes that the university should not be, cannot be all things to all people nor ought it to assume responsibility for meeting the total spectrum of adult education needs. Its obligation, rather, is to cooperate actively with all other agencies engaged in continuing education in order to ensure adequate service to all segments of the community. Specifically, this requires that the university should sustain and extend formal representation and participation in those associations committed to the fostering of continuing education. Other institutions, McMaster University (1970 and 1976) among them, acknowledge the necessity to reconsider the relationship of work done by the university in continuing education to that undertaken by other institutions, notably the community colleges, a major mandate of which is the provision of general interest programs. In consequence of similar reviews, some universities have culled their programs of continuing education; others continue to compete to greater or lesser degree with community colleges with programs often parallel in content and level.

But while, in the main, there is acknowledgement that there ought to be cooperation among the various providers of continuing education, effective working models of effective inter-agency liaison are few. Government, it might be noted, which supports most of the agencies which provide continuing education with public funds has an obvious stake in economies which might be effected through cooperation. Adult learners—who are also voters—confronted with announcements of seemingly competitive continuing education offerings would welcome some assurance of cooperative planning among institutions which today offer them a seemingly competitive array of alternative subjects, levels and credentials.

How the university continuing education function should be financed seems rarely to have been discussed by Canadian universities, though the sums of money and the numbers of students involved have become substantial. With respect to credit courses, the common practice is to ensure they recover such costs as instructional honoraria, supplies, travel expenses and the salary of organizing staff but not such overhead items as rentals, library facilities, counseling services and the record work performed by the registrar. Noncredit programs, on the other hand, are invariably required to be wholly or mainly self-supporting, an arrangement which a University of Victoria report (1972) labels as "pernicious" because of its assumption that the education of youth is more important than the education of adults. There is little logic, the report declares, in the assumption that a year of schooling at the age of twenty is more beneficial than a year at age thirty or forty or sixty. Indeed, both the individual and society might well benefit from the learner's earlier entry into the labor force and his later return to education. A particular danger of the pressure to self-support of the continuing education function is the generation of what sociologist Burton R. Clark (1956) terms an "enrollment economy" in which the volume of education output and cost recovery methods take precedence over educational purpose and quality.

Three patterns in the financing of university continuing education are evident: that in which the continuing education division is budgeted to return a profit to the institution; that in which the division exists by it wits on what it can earn in fees or attract in grants; and that in which a partial subsidy, not necessarily the product of a formula, is provided by the institution. An occasional theme in university statements in this: that to enable the university to respond to public demand for continuing education service government itself must provide supplementary funds and not expect the institution to dip into its existing budget.* A sharply different view is that of Dalhousie University (1976) which argues that the university must make a commitment to continuing education, establish the internal arrangements necessary to provide a comprehensive program, calculate the costs and apply the necessary financial restrictions. A generally acceptable rationale for the financing of continuing education—one which concedes the significance of the function and recognizes the public's right of access to the university—has yet to emerge.

University reports display little recognition of the education of adults as an emerging field of study nor do they speculate on what

---

*This notion reflects an 1894 Statute of the University of Toronto which stipulated that "no part of the expense incurred for teaching or examining done at 'local centers' of instruction, or for secretarial work done under the authority of the Committee, or for other purpose connected with University Extension shall be a charge on the ordinary revenue of the University."

contribution a professionally trained leadership might make to this university function. There are exceptions: McMaster University (1970) concedes the need to improve the instructional skill of teachers of adults while Dalhousie University (1976) (which offers a graduate degree in continuing education) proposes a closer relationship within the university between those *training* continuing educators and those *providing* continuing education to adults.

If formal training in the education of adults to the graduate level constitute its central component, there is a vacuum in the professional leadership of university continuing education in Canada. Within university continuing education divisions, it would appear, the orientation of present existing leadership leans toward the immediate and the practical, to the mechanics of administration rather than to a body of underlying theory respecting the education of adults. University continuing educators have themselves urged the appointment to university continuing education positions of those trained to the graduate level in this field (Canadian Association for University Continuing Education 1970). A University of Lethbridge report proposes that professional appointees to the staff of its continuing education division should have academic qualifications comparable to those of the faculty, hold professional rank, and be subject to the same institutional reward system (Selman & Sheats 1968, 16).

Apart from the universities, other related agencies have examined aspects of the university continuing education function. Their collective views about continuing education drawn from six major reports supplement the disparate explorations of the universities.

As Pilkington's (1974) well-documented study demonstrates, The Association of Universities and Colleges of Canada (AUCC), in the seven decades of its existence, has largely ignored continuing education. But a 1977 policy study, "The Role of the University," initiated by the AUCC and prompted in part by three related factors — the financial restrictions imposed on Canadian institutions, the tapering off in the size of the eighteen-to-twenty-four-year-old group, and the projected demographic shifts in Canada over the next twenty years — devotes a dozen of its pages to continuing education. The first of its six recommendations with respect to continuing education proposes that, jointly with adult learners, universities should study the mechanisms and structures required in order to respond to the variety of needs of the various clienteles for continuing education. A second recommendation, "that in each province a group established under provincial government auspices to coordinate and regulate continuing education for the province, to supervise certification procedures, to recommend and allocate funding . . ." astonishes in its atypical acceptance of external control of a university function.

The same study recommends that degree programs on a part-time basis, both graduate and undergraduate, be considered as much a responsibility of the university as full-time programs, and that sufficient resources be allocated to part-time programs to ensure that they will be scheduled in a systematic way. Two subsequent recommendations deal with finance. The first invites federal government assistance to part-time students under the Canada Students Loans Program; the second, invested with fascinating political ramifications, recommends that provincial governments provide funds to community groups for the purchase of educational services from postsecondary institutions.

A difficulty not yet resolved, yet inviting attention, is the establishment of some *modus vivendi* between universities and colleges who are competitors in the provision of continuing education. Hence this final recommendation of the AUCC Report: that there be planning and coordination between universities and community colleges in continuing education in the same geographical area, so that each will offer the courses that are appropriate to its function and avoid duplication.

One of few agency studies which is truly national in scope, "Continuing Education in Canada," conducted by Stager and Thomas for the University of Toronto's Institute for Policy Analyses in 1972, deals with the university's special role in the provision of continuing education. The "mature student" admission clause in Canadian universities, an arbitrarily defined category, permits adults admission usually to the first year of an undergraduate program without conventional admission requirements. This policy, the report observes, represents a major modification to the pyramidal character which has dominated Canadian education in which admission to any level was invariably dictated by performance at the immediately previous level. Until recently, the student leaving the education system could only re-enter at the point of exit, regardless of what he might have experienced or learned in the meantime, a circumstance now claimed to be both inadequate and unjust. Indeed, the report speculates, some means of ensuring flexibility in connecting genuine educational achievement in a wide variety of private educational experiences to the legitimizing process of institutions must be found if that process is to continue acceptable to the public.

The bulk of this report documents in detail the rapid growth of part-time credit studies while a relatively small section of it deals with part-time noncredit work. Both have extended the university remarkably in both time and space. Of interest are contrasts drawn between Western and Eastern Canadian institutions in their provision of continuing education. The former were established by provincial legislatures and, influenced by the American Morrill Act of 1862, have given greater attention to the extension function. The eastern universities, which originated largely as private institutions, have taken a considerably more conservative view of their responsibilities for the education of adults. Their expectation, moreover, of the continuing education operation was that it should fund itself or even generate revenue for the institution. (This may account for the important place accorded formal noncredit certificate programs designed by national associations concerned with office management, real estate, accounting and personnel work, but offered under the aegis of universities to which they represent a rich source of dependable funds.) The report predicts that the demand for informal noncredit services provided by universities will not diminish but in fact will increase as adult learners substitute short-term noncredit learning activities for the pursuit of degrees, certificates or diplomas.

Its final observation notes the rudimentary character of research into continuing education in Canada, the lack of data descriptive and analytical of the field, and its consequences: the want of a comprehensive public policy with respect to continuing education; and the tenuous relationships between the institutions providing it.

A 1977 field study prepared for the Government of Alberta, *Adult Education as a Field of Study and Practice: Strategies for Development*, examines the potential of the university to develop continuing education as a field (Campbell 1977b). Because the variety of agencies organized to meet adult learning needs is large and increasing, because the predicted rate of growth in the number of adult learners is high, and because the future clientele will be better educated (and thus more sophisticated in its demands) a strong *prima facie* case can be made for university development of continuing education as a field of study as a matter of priority. The task of upgrading the competence of a large group of practitioners, of creating a corps of trained, full-time professionals, it is argued, is a natural extension of university responsibility. In the organization of such training, the key issues are perceived to be these: the format of training with its implications for credentials; the provision of that training in such a way as to ensure ready access to it by field workers; and the integration of training with research and field practice. The training provided by the university, the report concludes, should be tied to field practice under the direction of professionally-prepared, experienced, continuing educators supported by an adequate stock of learning materials. Continuing education development, as this and other reports note, is impeded by the lack of support afforded it through research and by the lack of mechanisms for its dissemination. Indeed, it would be short-sighted and even irresponsible for university institutions to make plans for the training of continuing education workers without coincidentally preparing to mount and sustain an ongoing program of research.

Reported in this work is a field study of the structure of provision of continuing education in Alberta which confirms that continuing education is an increasingly significant part of the province's educational provision, that the demand for training in continuing education is substantial, that there is considerable consensus both with respect to preferred training content and as to how training should be organized and presented.

Among the more thoughtful and prescient position papers on continuing education in the Canadian university, one which gives coherence to the subject is that prepared in 1970 by the Canadian Association of Departments of Extension and Summer Schools in Universities (now known as the Canadian Association for University Continuing Education or CAUCE). Certain features of that society the university will serve in the future, it argues, which have clear implications for continuing education are already apparent. Because of the advances in communications, information can move universally and instantaneously. Thus, an essential task of continuing education will be to help people select and apply available information to serve their purposes. Second, because complex technology has consequences in equally complex ecological outcomes, a responsibility of education will be to create awareness of these outcomes and possible solutions to the problems they generate. Out of the increasing complexity of organizational life has emerged a fresh awareness of the potential of man and his individuality. Helping to develop and focus his potential is a third task of education.

The CAUCE report postulates three basic assumptions. First, the goals of university continuing education are not apart from the nature of the goals of the university as a whole. A second conviction is that the adult learner comes to his education with a given structure of experience, with a definite commitment to learning, with specific learning needs, and with the desire to link his learning to his life experience. Third is a conception of education as a lifelong process in which the traditional segmentation of education experiences becomes dysfunctional. Thus, bridges need to be built between the elementary, secondary, postsecondary and continuing education enterprises. Flowing out of these assumptions, the report continues, are these guides to university continuing education practice:

- university continuing education programs should be based on the standards of an academic discipline and should also reflect the increasingly interdisciplinary nature of much of university work
- the continuing education function should be viewed as the responsibility of the university as a whole and not merely as one assigned to a division of the institution
- no more than are other approaches to education, university continuing education should not be required to support itself financially; good education costs money and excellence should not be sacrificed to expediency
- programs of university continuing education should reflect the educational needs of the community, the character of the university, and the realities of the environment
- community-related programs should reflect the judgment and experience of adult leaders in the community. (The Secretary of State for Canada (Pelletier 1968), makes the point that "[it would be] interesting for the university to propose definite ways of breaking out of the academic aristocracy and ensuring an

increased presence of society itself at the deliberating table where the future of the university is being planned.")
- the university should give leadership to the development of continuing education through refining the theoretical and conceptual bases of the field.

Recommendations as to the operation of the university continuing education function conclude the CAUCE report. While universities will continue to fulfill their traditional roles of generating, preserving and disseminating knowledge, the key responsibility of its continuing education thrust ought to be "the organized application of information to end results" (Drucker 1968). In contemporary society, that knowledge will be directed to an adult constituency concerned with preparation for jobs, with mid-career changes of occupation, with personal development, and with improvement in the quality of the physical and social environment. Because the demand for programs and for educational experiences which are informal and community-based will expand rapidly, there should be within the university an identified core of staff members competent to initiate and conduct programs of community service. What should accompany the university's provision of continuing education is ready access by adult learners to adequate professional counselling facilities, policies which facilitate the use of the university's libraries by part-time students, and procedures which will encourage the entry of mature students to degree and nondegree programs. To reflect its present and future significance and enable it to achieve its potential, university continuing education should be headed by an appointee at the vice-presidential level and its curriculum and policies should be the object of review by academic councils. The subsidy provided university continuing education programs should be at a level equal to that provided conventional university work; and faculty contributions to institutional programs of continuing education should be negotiated at the time of their initial appointment on a regular load basis rather than subsequently on an overload basis.

Another national review bearing directly on university continuing education is the Statistics Canada document, *The Class of 2001* (Clark, Deveraux & Zsigmond 1979) which projects extraordinary swings in student numbers through every level of the education system. The post-secondary age group—those from eighteen to twenty-four years of age—increased 87 percent between 1961 and 1978 to 3.2 million and was projected to reach its peak for the century in 1982 after which it will decline by 21 percent to 2.7 million in 1996. Provincial variations are expected: the relative figure for Quebec, for example, is expected to be 32 percent and that in Alberta 11 percent. In another perspective, the group of Canadian adults between the ages of twenty-five and forty-four which in 1980 is projected to number 3,481,700, will, by the year 2000, have expanded to 4,518,200, an increase of 30 percent (Statistics Canada 1974). While these data warrant cautious interpretation (since many factors clearly influence postsecondary enrollment) the rollercoaster demographics forecast can scarcely be ignored. One impact of a decline (should it materialize as projected is this decade) in the conventional student body—currently the basis for institutional funding—is direct and possibly brutal. Projected expenditures per student in constant dollars would appear to increase as enrollment falls while fixed costs of the university will not decline: tenure impeded cost-cutting and the number of nonteaching positions tends to be relatively insensitive to enrollment fluctuations. A further unhappy consequence of a decline in the conventional student body (one already notably evident in the United States) may be sharp competition for the dwindling number of potential conventional students, a contest which may exacerbate interinstitutional relations.

Not yet widely recognized is the opportunity presented by the projected but deferred decline in the conventional student body to seek out and serve a constituency of adult learners. This is the theme explored in an Ontario study by Pike (1978), "Part-Time Undergraduate Studies in Ontario": that universities should move beyond the traditional view which limits education to the first two decades of life and initiate those reforms required to facilitate part-time learning. Two factors will motivate such change. The first is enhanced citizen awareness of the right of access to universities. Pike's assessment of new public sensitivity to its rights in higher education prompts his warning that universities are beholden to redefine the role they will play in this period of rapid social change or face a crisis of public confidence. The second is institutional self-interest reflected in efforts to make up for diminishing enrollments (and funds) from traditional sources by attracting a more varied clientele. A significant notion in this study is that of "generational inequality." Pike argues the existence of a substantial pool of older adults of all social backgrounds—their scholastic abilities unmeasured—for whom participation in any form of post-secondary study after completing high school was denied, a wastage of talent consistently reported in previous surveys. Furthermore, the university demonstrates a substantial social bias in favor of the upper middle-classes among school leavers; the probability is that there are still relatively large numbers of lower-class and lower-middle-class youth in the province with the mental ability to profit from university who do not go on to full-time undergraduate studies. Despite the existence of special and mature admissions programs, the report concludes, part-time undergraduate studies in Ontario are not a major instrument of social and occupational upward mobility for those in manual occupations. Universities in metropolitan areas serving large populations, the author suggests, will have little difficulty in the future in continuing to attract more than sufficient numbers of part-time students. But the trend, Pike suggests, is a shift in the social role of metropolitan universities as agencies of upward social mobility for a predominantly Canadian-born, Anglo-Saxon clientele to agencies of upward social mobility for Ontario's sizeable white and nonwhite minority immigrant groups.

Two principal features, Pike notes, mark the current provision of opportunities for part-time study: the anomalies and inequities faced by the part-time learner in comparison to full-time students; and the low status accorded part-time learners, constantly reinforced and symbolized by their instruction on a stipend-based, staff-overload system by those appearing "less to be cultivating the vineyard of learning than operating a mining claim." In short, educational opportunities for part-time students are inferior to those open to full-time students and, as this report documents, the former, most of them adult learners, face these problems:
- the range of courses outside regular day hours is too limited and instructional time allotted to part-time students is often curtailed
- too few of the senior academic staff teach evening courses; overload teaching (which inhibits the proper planning of courses) by junior faculty members predominates; commitment by departments and individual faculty members to part-time students is insufficient
- part-time students do not have an effective advocate on the campus; academic counselling is inadequate or unavailable
- there is a widespread belief, proven or not, that part-time students produce inferior academic work

- part-time students rarely have social facilities available for their use
- a cost of instruction usually proportionately higher than that assessed full-time students.

As Winston Churchill observed, "Those who are possessed of a definite body of doctrine and of deeply rooted convictions upon it will be in a much better position to deal with the shifts and surprises of daily affairs than those who are merely taking short views, and indulging their natural impulses as they are evoked by what they read from day to day." Taken together, the analyses of university continuing education drawn from provincially-sponsored commission reports, from the examination of individual universities, and from the researches of agencies serving higher education can scarcely be said to provide such a "definite body of doctrine." In fact, research in Canada in university continuing education is neither extensive or complete; few elements of it are national in scope and little of it has an empirical base.

To be sure, it would be unrealistic to expect uniformity and a sense of common purpose among a range of university institutions so different in their history, their sense of mission, their resources and the community that they serve. What these studies point to is a common set of *issues* respecting the continuing education function which will be examined in the succeeding three chapters from these perspectives: continuing education program; its design and delivery; structure and policies for the function.

3 University Continuing Education Program

University continuing education program is shaped by a mix of beliefs about institutional purposes, about priorities in the learning needs within its constituency of adult learners, and about how adults learn. What follows is a sketch of the five chief segments of university continuing education program and an assessment of the forces which influence each.

Two propositions are introductory. The first is that continuing education is not to be lumped together with community work or social service. Its justification is as education; its claim to support is as a system of teaching and learning (Lawson 1975). The second is that university continuing education should respond—in a balanced way—to this range of needs:

PERSONAL: remedial or compensatory education; the extension of formal education to satisfy personal objectives.

ECONOMIC: occupational re-orientation: preparation for new jobs and, subsequently, for new responsibilities in those jobs.

VOCATIONAL: attainment of initial vocational qualifications and, subsequently, training to offset their obsolescence.

SOCIAL: adaptation to changing circumstances including social attitudes and habits; an awareness of personal and social ethics and values; the development of social understanding and skills;

fulfilment of particular roles in the community (Open University 1976, 23-24).

Despite the breadth of this range of needs, the reality is that university continuing education provision is biased towards the development of marketable skills and the attainment of certification (OECD 1976a). Coincidentally, organizations representing the arts complain that continuing education provides few learning opportunities in the realm of culture and the arts, and meanwhile, the scientific community deplores the lack of public understanding of the role of science and its impact on society.

Part-time Courses for University Credit

Adult part-time learners in credit and noncredit courses have today become the majority of students in Canadian universities. Remarkably, this phenomenon has gone largely unnoticed on the campus though it nonetheless marks a significant change. Equally remarkable, it is not a consequence of predetermined educational principles or a response to stated public policy; it is not aimed towards the accomplishment of some set of expressed objectives; and it has developed according to no systematic criteria. Like Topsy, it has just grown. Yet the continuing education of adults represents as popular a mass movement as postsecondary education has ever experienced (National Advisory Council on Extension and Continuing Education 1975).

The indifference of universities to this phenomenon is the more curious in the light of the post-war invasion of North American campuses by thousands of veterans. Despite initial predictions that they would fail, these adult learners proved to be serious, hard-working, well-behaved, productive students (and, indeed, it was this government-initiated experiment which moved universities out of their relative obscurity of prewar years.) Today, the expansion in the numbers of adult learners seeking degrees through part-time credit offers universities a parallel opportunity. American institutions for their part have been vigorous, even frantic, in their efforts to attract this new client group through campaigns variously labelled marketing, recruitment or audience development. Publicity approaches which a decade ago would have been deemed undignified — newspaper, radio and television advertising, the production of special brochures, recruitment by teams of alumni — are today part of the competitive scramble for adult students. Moreover, universities seek heightened visibility through the reorganization of curriculum and through such devices as mini-courses, satellite campuses, relaxed admission standards, educational brokerage, special programs in new areas (such as women's studies, literacy education, drug addiction and alcoholism counselling), the introduction of modular courses and wholesale changes in scheduling.

Canadian universities have not been obliged to compete in such fashion for survival. But within their potential constituency of adult learners is open questioning of such traditional assumptions of the university as these:
- the requirement of in-person attendance on campus
- the requirement that courses be offered only by an institutional staff member
- the assumption that education must fit within a given timeframe such as a term or session or period of years
- the assumption of the university of the sanctity of the content of the courses it develops
- the assumption that conventional classroom study is the only valid way of acquiring knowledge and skills appropriate to credit towards a degree (Small 1975).

Institutional planning to accomodate the education of adults is not without its difficulties. In the first place, this basically different market requires different approaches for which there is little in the way of past experience to guide. The exact nature and extent of demand for part-time education is unclear (National Advisory Council on Extension and Continuing Education 1975, 13). As has been noted, certain components of the traditional approach to university education — full-time residency, campus-centered offerings, day-time scheduling — are unhelpful to existing and potential adult constituents. The diversity of this new clientele obliges a parallel diversity of institutional responses with respect, for example, to teaching formats, instructional centers, information services and counselling. Still another problem for the university in the provision of education to adults on a part-time basis is that the demand for it shifts rapidly in response to changes in the economy or in the labor force or as a result of pressures exerted by business, professional, governmental or social groups.

Within the institution there are other points of difficulty. Much of teaching in university continuing education for credit is conducted on the basis of faculty overload. Those pressed to undertake such instructional responsibilities may grudge the time lost to research on which, in the institutional reward system, their promotion may chiefly depend. Indeed, assignment to the instruction part-time credit courses on or off the campus may be seen as relegation to an academic Siberia. It is not the more senior members of the faculty who provide instruction; most of part-time credit courses are conducted by junior staff for extra income, a kind of moonlighting. The larger institution, of course, could avoid the problems inherent in overload staffing by recruiting an instructional cadre paralleling the regular academic staff but separate from it. But this approach creates an awkward caste system within academic ranks and in times of budget stringency, that solution is not viable.

Other organizational problems, many of them remediable, inhibit the adult learner's access to credit courses. The services readily available to the full-time student—counselling, placement and child care—may be denied to the part-time learner. Registration hours, the opportunity to consult professors, and even the acquisition of basic information about the university's program are all hurdles which frustrate and anger eager adult students (well aware that their tax dollars support the institution). What often vexes students attempting university credit studies at off-campus centers is lack of access to library service. Understandably, librarians and staff wish to keep library holdings intact; on the other hand, the student without adequate book resources is disadvantaged and his learning experience is rendered less rich. The year to year scheduling of course offerings may be unsystematic and leave part-time credit students uncertain whether prerequisite courses or others required in their area of concentration will be available at convenient times or at all.

To some students, the distinction made between part-time degree studies and formal noncredit work seems artificial; certainly, the considerably higher fee usually paid for the latter is a source of grievance to the adult learner (University of Alberta 1976). According to student critics, too, the narrowness, formality and inflexibility of part-time undergraduates degree requirements do not provide the optimal quality of education. Some academic administrators feel they may have a point and recommend that to provide flexibility, universities should allow adults to accumulate credits in many ways: by recognizing courses taken earlier at other institutions; by examinations and assessment of learning through life experience; by accepting credits earned on field projects or in evening and summer classes or through extension and correspondence. True, something may be lost by combining credits in so many ways; but as some educators now admit, much is to be gained by exposure to different learning experiences (Harrington 1977).

The summer school could well play a larger role in the education of adults. Invented for teachers and still largely dominated by them, it offers a more relaxed atmosphere than is sometimes evident in traditional night classes. Conceivably, cooperative planning with the community could result in university provision of special educational services aimed at those in business and industry, professional groups, government and community organizations. Alternatively, the summer school might very effectively serve adult learners were it to link its programs to independent study and correspondence work undertaken by students other times of the year.

But the most serious problem is that of ensuring equitable access to all citizen groups to the university. Through its credit and non-credit programs, the university largely serves those already high on the socio-economic scale. Thus—and this is a serious concern—it acts to broaden the already wide gaps between rich and poor. A current U.S. study of adult education confirms that much of adult education is now frankly elitist, that equal opportunity as a goal has become ever more distant. But while the educational gap between the "haves" and the "have-nots" is increasing, there would now appear to be more opportunity for disadvantaged young people to gain access to college than for older adults to continue the kinds of education that would be useful to them (Cross 1978). Information centers, "brokering services" in the current jargon, offer realistic hope for linking learning needs to learning resources.

Pike's 1970 and 1978 studies examine citizen access to Ontario universities and sketch the clientele served. Only about 15 percent of full-time undergraduates are over the age of twenty-four compared to 75 percent of part-time students. Part-time students are older and many of them are saddled with the responsibilities of job and family; yet they tend to be treated as traditional students and so face real barriers in continuing their education. What this study invites of universities is a commitment to the education of adults in terms which reflect these students' adult status and responsibilities. Specifically, this suggests possible modifications of curricula, the examination of some means of providing financial assistance and the review of institutional schedules. But perhaps the most difficult step is that of changing faculty attitudes and gaining recognition of this certainty: that the clientele for higher education will never again be as relatively homogeneous as the eighteen-to-twenty-four-years old once served. In short, as the American Association for Higher Education predicts, policies for this new majority will be shaped by very different social and educational priorities which will demand more flexibility of universities (Eddy 1978).

Professional and Paraprofessional Studies

Education and training related to job or career is by far the largest element of university continuing education program. In virtually all vocations today, an initial training marks only a preliminary preparation. Of this substantial segment of continuing education program, part is linked specifically to the established professions and particularly to medicine, law and accounting. The remainder, either through extensive, well-established curricula or through an array of unrelated, specialized *ad hoc* courses, is more generally aimed at paraprofessionals and those in business or industry.

What is true of continuing education in general is also true of continuing professional education: the two factors most closely linked with participation in it are the level of formal education and income. It is the already successful and innovative who are the more likely to participate in it.

A variety of reasons for participating in continuing professional education can be identified:
- to keep up with the new knowledge required to perform responsibly in a chosen career
- to master new conceptions of the career itself as its orientation shifts
- to keep abreast of changes in the basic disciplines underlying the profession
- to enable preparation for changes in a personal career line

- to maintain a freshness of outlook on one's work . . . the possibilities of approaching it in different ways
- to enable the professional to concentrate his skills responsibly and constructively in a society whose problems he knows and understands
- to retain the will and capacity to learn (Houle 1978).

Several factors today shape the expansion of continuing professional education. Both the public and the professionals themselves are sharply aware of the need to maintain professional competence. Government desires to protect the public by requiring relicensure examinations. Also, there is the view that, the expansion in the professional's stock of knowledge aside, skill in the processes of learning and enquiry is eminently desirable in the professional (Knox 1975).

The pattern of continuing professional education has undergone several transitions. There was early recognition that, after some years in practice and with the accumulation of field experience, a refresher course was desirable. With the rapid acceleration of knowledge particularly in the sciences stimulated by World War II, casual refresher education was succeeded by the concept of "continuing education" of which the seminar, residential conference, intensive short courses and self-study units were elements. Currently, there is recognition that a university degree marks only the beginning of the education of a professional, that the "half-life" of professional knowledge may be as low as several years. Thus, on the horizon is "re-education": the periodic reassessment of the whole of a profession in order to separate and discard areas of earlier knowledge. Complicating the lifelong learning process in the professions is that an expanding body of knowledge has forced a proliferation of specialization; yet the professional must remain enough of a generalist to comprehend the whole of his field if he is to make sound decisions. What makes the matter even more awkward to handle is the increasing overlap of professional fields and thus the requirement of interdisciplinary and multidisciplinary study (Frandson 1978 approx.).

Beyond the technical-professional element of continuing professional education is another obvious but often overlooked consideration: that professional education should combine technical skills with liberal education. Professional skills are not exercised in a vacuum; but are applied in a social setting. Whether professionals will contribute optimally to society will depend largely upon their knowledge and understanding of that society and their appreciation of its particular problems and requirements. Not only must professionals keep abreast of their own field, if they are to serve the public with maximum skill and effectiveness, they must also be informed about and sensitive to shifts in society itself and changes in its values, expectations, needs and resources. In Canada, moreover, the professional ought to be able to communicate with others in either of the country's official languages (Symons 1975).

Almost all professional organizations have explored and adopted different approaches to continuing professional education. Some view it as a responsibility of the individual; voluntary participation in it may be encouraged and recognized but the requirement of participation in it is shunned. Others stipulate participation in continuing education as a condition of maintaining membership in a professional association. Continuing education through a program prescribed and regulated by government may be established as a mandatory requirement. Or a professional association, in consultation with its members and the public, having devised suitable standards of practice and determined procedures to assess competence, may present its recommendations to local or provincial organizations for their consideration as a basis for relicensure (Knox 1975).

Three mechanisms for establishing continuing education within the professions appear to be most favored: self-directed study with its concomitant of personal responsibility to self, profession and clientele; the periodic re-determination of competence evidenced by some kind of evaluation; and mandated, formal continuing education (Frandson 1978). But whatever the mechanism chosen, it will be recognized that a variety of groups have a stake in continuing professional education. There is the university institution whose interests can be described in fiscal or policy or power terms. Within the university itself are the professional schools each with its special concerns, a group of institutional administrators with their priorities, and an extension division with its operational apparatus in place. Each of these will take different views of the same problems—and bring different talents to their solution. The universities are not the only institutions interested in continuing professional education. The community colleges, arguing their availability and accessibility and keenly aware of the enhanced image that such service could give them, have a clear interest. The professional associations themselves, national or provincial, have an obvious interest in continuing professional education. There are the private educational entrepreneurs with a higher profile, thus far, in the United States than in Canada, who covet the lucrative market presented by professional groups. Finally, representing the consumer are legislatures which are largely responsible for the laws and regulations which govern professional groups. Working hand-in-hand with government is a variety of boards and regulatory agencies (Stern 1976). What seems clear is that the university, as a central player in this vital new area of higher education (though it can overlook none of the others) is presented with new obligations and new opportunities to which it must give careful study.

Permeating any approach to continuing professional education is the issue of rights to its control: the rights of the profession to control professional mission, goals and objectives; the rights of individuals within professional ranks to control their own lives; the rights of control by agencies outside the profession such as government and those private bodies which fund research or provide training facilities; and the rights of consumers, increasingly more vociferous, who may be represented by voluntary organizations or by government boards. The scramble for pride of place among these competitors is aptly illustrated in such issues as malpractice, client relationships and economic or racial discrimination (Frandson 1978).

What is desirable in the content, delivery and promotion of program in continuing professional education has been examined in such studies as that undertaken by the University of Massachusetts: "The educational activities desired are short, topical, well developed, lively presentations thoroughly focussed as to subject, but not lacking in professional breadth, are based on the stated desires of the professionals, offered at convenient times and places and structured to enhance their social functionality. . . . The likely avenues of delivery of services are a combination of centralized and decentralized residential presentations. . . . The associations, its publications and meetings offer the most suitable, readily available avenue for promotion" (Donnelly n.d.). But striking weaknesses in continuing professional education of which the university ought to be aware are reported. Many continuing professional education courses are so absurdly short as to be virtually without value. Moreover, they are more narrow, by a factor of two or three, than professional courses given for degree credit on the campus. Technical information is likely to take precedence over an understanding of changes in the character of the society in which the professional is practicing. There are other charges: that continuing professional education remains an upper-crust affair chiefly benefiting upper-income professionals; and that women meet with discrimination in their pursuit of it (Harrington 1977; and LeBreton & others 1979).

Where responsibility for the continuing education of the professional is best placed on the campus will vary with the institution and the profession itself. Whichever university agency manages it, these are the practical issues inherent in providing it:

- How best are linkages developed with professional associations, regulatory bodies and consumer interests? How can the university remain open to these multiple, changing, and likely conflicting interests?
- What design of continuing professional education will ensure that it is consistent with the learners' needs, learning styles and time limitations?
- How can continuing professional education programs which reflect the geographic realities of the community and its intellectual resources, and which meet both the wants *and* needs of learners be developed and delivered?
- How can the university appropriately serve the needs of the consumer of the continuing professional education product? In what respects ought continuing professional education be open to public accountability? (Rockhill 1976).

What is essential to the success of the continuing education program is that its design reflects what is known about how best adults learn. The specialist trained in continuing education is indispensible to the solution of the complex problems posed in the continuing education of adults.

In engaging in continuing professional education, the university is not only placed in relationship to a variety of other interested groups but is inevitably party to a set of connected public issues. One of the most vexing of these is that of compulsion in continuing education in the professions towards which, in the United States, there is evidence of a trend. There, mandatory continuing legal education requiring that lawyers spend at least fifteen hours a year taking approved courses is an element in an education program which has already been approved by six State bar associations with a dozen about to follow suit (*Saturday Review* 1978). Among those professions in which it appears that continuing education is more likely to be made compulsory are those which are older, those which are stronger, those which are health-related, and those in which private practice is the dominant mode. Compulsion is repugnant to the academic mind. While the American Association for Higher Education (1979) agrees that professional groups should support vigorous voluntary programs reinforced where feasible by self-assessment mechanisms, it states categorically that there is no evidence that continuing education ensures continued competence. Tempting though the mandatory requirement may be in regulatory policy, universities are well advised to be cautious of it. There is a related problem in relicensure connected to compulsory continuing professional education in which, at least indirectly, the university may necessarily become involved. Since the pressure for continuing professional education comes mainly from off the campus—from practicing professionals, companies, government agencies and trade associations—the control of continuing professional education, even though sited on the campus, may slip out of the hands of the university. While the rhetoric of the profession, one critic claims, is one of service to the consumer, the reality is that of self-service by professionals in a drive for control over an occupational field (Rockhill 1976). A Canadian analysis of the trend towards compulsory continuing education in the professions notes that the Province of Quebec in its Professional Code of 1973 has taken a dramatic step towards the regulation of professions by making it clear that the role of the professional body is to protect the public and not to serve as a self-preserving lobby group (Linder 1973).

Liberal and General Studies

The initial thrust, the *raison d'etre* of adult education in Canada, the United States and Britain was the study of the humanities: that education, based on Socrates' assumption that the unexamined life is not worth living, which seeks to determine and clarify human needs and values.

Today, the humanities account for only a small fraction of registrations; it is professional and vocational studies which dominate university continuing education course offerings. To the more pessimistic observers, liberal education is largely dead. "Its humanistic heartbeat has failed, and rigor mortis is setting in throughout the giant higher educational system. The humanistic ideal of involving the whole man in the quest for order and beauty through the ennobling exposure to other men's accomplishments has been mostly replaced by the training of task-oriented technicians" (Billington 1968). In the eyes of students, the university has been debased to a tool, a passport to success, which offers no inspiration, no vision of higher motive for life or a vast new world (Murchland 1976).

Indeed, it does seem clear that continuing education programs offered in the humanities are unattractive to adult students. There are several possible reasons. The vocational side of university continuing education through its contacts with professional associations, business and industry, has a foot in the community. But in contrast—one of the anomalies of higher education—while universities are constantly expanding their community outreach in the vocations, the humanities remain, for the most part, aloof from the sweaty day-to-day concerns of ordinary people (Lenx 1976, 2). Clark Kerr refers to the "guild mentality" of those in the social sciences and humanities, an attitude which insulates them from society. Without that vital interaction, he charges, they become preservers of tradition sheltering in the confines of an approved body of knowledge, a posture which others have termed "privatization." There is another factor. Adults interested in noncredit liberal studies courses wish to learn what interests them and not what is stipulated in a degree program. They are seeking learning which is stimulating—and even enjoyable; they do not want to become apprentices to a discipline (which is increasingly the orientation of the university department). They want to enhance, even change the direction of, their lives in a fundamental way. They are searching for that which is directly relevant and meaningful to their lives.* To Britain's most eloquent spokesman for adult education,

---

*A series of liberal arts skills, defined as "transferable, functional abilities that are required in many different problem-solving and task-oriented situations" is set out in Paul Brun, "76 career-related liberal arts skills," American Association for Higher Education, *Bulletin*, October, 1981, p. 9.

"the purpose of an adult education worthy of the name is not merely to impart reliable information important though that is. It is still more to foster the intellectual vitality to master and use it, so that knowledge becomes, not a burden to be borne or a possession to be prized, but a stimulus to constructive thought and an inspiration to action" (Tawney 1966, 88). What change will such study create in me, the adult student asks? What will it tell me about myself in relation to work or to other people or the community or to the cosmos?

The array of noncredit offerings of the university in liberal studies suggests no discernible pattern, little in the way of relationship of one element to another, and only infrequent opportunity to pursue a subject at successive levels. The residual impression is not that of a program based on an obvious philosophy but rather of a parade of isolated events patched together in the hope that some may engage public interest. While the kind of basic philosophy which underlies a conventional degree program in the liberal arts cannot wholly meet adult needs in noncredit studies, it at least suggests that kind of coherence which continuing education programs in liberal studies now lack. Harvard's core curriculum, for example, offers a basic philosophy and useful guidelines to the university in its continuing education programs in liberal studies:

> An educated person must be able to think and write clearly and effectively. . . .
> An educated person should have a critical appreciation of the ways in which we gain knowledge . . . of what kinds of knowledge exist in certain important areas, how such knowledge is acquired, how it is deployed, and what it might mean to [him] personally.
> An educated person . . . cannot be ignorant of other cultures and other times. It is no longer possible to conduct our lives without reference to the wider world within which we live. . . .
> An educated person is expected to have some understanding of, and experience in thinking about, moral and ethical problems . . . which enable [him] to make discriminating moral choices. . . .
> An educated individual should have achieved depth in some field of knowledge [since] cumulative learning is an effective way to develop . . . powers of reasoning and analysis (*CAUT Bulletin* 1979, 13).

There are other problems in university provision of liberal and general studies. There often appears a lack of coordination among the differing providers of continuing general education and an absence of an appropriate and clearly defined institutional role. This is understandable because continuing education is deemed marginal, and its operation is not usually planned at the policy-making levels of the institution (Selman 1978). A serious fault of noncredit general studies within the university continuing education program is the inclusion in it of courses of doubtful academic value. Quite justifiably, the critics of such programs ask what rationale there is for university-based courses on "How To Be Successful" or "Ways of Getting Your 'Self' Together" or others which seem no more than spin-offs from current best sellers. The contrast such courses offer to what was typical in the general studies curriculum of three decades ago—the discussion of reason or free will or the destiny of man in Hutchins' Great Books Program—is profound. The consequences of offering such educational junk-food are real and negative. Such offerings invite the contemptuous dismissal by academics of the whole of the continuing education effort (and on their cooperation the enterprise depends); the program loses credibility in the eyes of the public; and, most important, the zeal of continuing educators themselves, their sense of mission, is diminished (Campbell 1979).

Some solutions have been suggested for the revival of liberal studies from its almost moribund condition. It is argued that if the liberal studies are to be restored to flourishing health they will have to "go public"—to move in from the margins of contemporary life to the vital center. To this end—connecting liberal studies with vital questions in the minds of people—a variety of processes and techniques might be employed for improving communication between academics and the public. Teaching techniques might be examined, and the role of film and other audiovisual devices explored (Lenz 1976). Another avenue particularly suitable to university continuing education divisions and urged by Symons (1975) is to blend a liberal education with its goal of creating a humanistic society with technical training. Still another approach to the improvement of noncredit general studies lies in upgrading the competence of continuing educators themselves: those responsible for assessing adult student needs, designing programs, implementing, administering and, finally, evaluating them (Selman 1978; Frandson 1978a; and Campbell 1977).

Community Development

Community development is that area of program concerned with the direct involvement of the university in the affairs of the community. Its rationale: that the community can be helped to adapt to change; that through study and leadership, the environment can be modified and human settlements made more congenial. Not well understood on the campus, it is defined as an effort "to discover ways of helping communities to help themselves through the study and efforts of their citizens. [Through projects which involve] . . . a new kind of extension education—education for all, education for action on a wide front, education that is democratic in nature and education that comes to grips with the realities that people have to face daily in the homes and communities in which they live" (National University Extension Association 1946, 5).

There are three specific aims of community development. First is an analysis of the components of the "community": that group of persons who interact on the basis of common knowledge, attachments and sentiments rather than through their connection to the business demands of the metropolis. Second is a strengthening of the sense of community held by a neighborhood through identifying its values and the encouragement of its democratic processes. A third aim is that of enabling a decision to act—the "action-solution" so called—which may focus of any condition of community life: its economic structure or sanitation or school system or recreation.

Macpherson's view (1970, 22) of the role of university as critic provides a conceptual base for the examination of university engagement in community development. Society, he suggests, has a right to expect the university to perform social functions; one appropriate to the institution is diagnosis. What a sick society needs most is diagnosis of its malfunctioning: ecological, physiological, economic, psychological, political and moral. It needs diagnosis not just of its mechanisms but of its values. Likening the university

to the jester of old—in this instance, a kind of multiple fool—
Macpherson argues that the task of the university is to strip the
pretensions from society's modern courtiers: businessmen cloaked
in the virtue of free enterprise who scheme to use the favors of
government to increase profits or labor leaders who exercise a
minority's tyranny or professional groups which see a perfect identity between their economic self-interest and the needs of society.
This is not a new ideal. The iconoclastic Abraham Flexner argued
a half-century ago that universities—those within them that is—
must maintain contact with the real world, must take an objective
position in reference to social and political and economic
phenomena—but at the same time must remain irresponsible. The
university in short is fundamentally a critical institution with an
obligation to give guidance and direction to society.

Macpherson's conception limits the critical role of the university
to the diagnosis of society. But beyond diagnosis lies prescription
and, subsequently, treatment in which the patient is the community. The basic thesis of this treatment, which is the community
development thrust of the university, is that environments can be
changed and that properly trained persons, drawn from on or off
the campus, and functioning as facilitators, questioners, analyzers
and probers—but not as leaders—can enable communities to accomplish beneficial developments or to resist detrimental changes.

Community development may pose a dilemma to the institution. It is one thing for individual academics privately to involve
themselves in community affairs; it is quite another for the institution itself to do so. The University of California's experiences in
the 1960s would seem to teach that if the academic community
chooses to use the university as a base for political action, if it attempts to identify the university with group causes or to mobilize
university prestige and resources to group ends, then the university
itself will inevitably become politicized. But strongly argued by the
Carnegie Foundation (1967, 14) is the contrary view that of all institutions in the nation, the university has the greatest responsibility to be a shaper of society, that it has an obligation to identify
social wrongs and take an aggressive lead in rectifying them.

The best known community development project in Canada is
the Antigonish movement, an initiative taken in the early 1930s by
St. Francis Xavier University. For two decades Dr. M. M. Coady,
its Director of Extension, encouraged the fishermen of that Nova

Scotia community in their efforts to mobilize basic facilities for adult education. In a very real sense, the university through its provision of informal education was a partner with the fishermen in devising and establishing cooperatives of producers to pack and market their fish. Among the consequences of this unusual intervention was the adoption by the industry of more scientific approaches to commercial fishing, the awakening of concern about public education generally and the neutralization of religious intolerance. Another notable achievement in Canadian community development similarly aided by the university were the Community Life Training Institutes in Alberta which spurred the development of cooperative business enterprises, county-wide hospitalization schemes and area school boards.

In North America, university involvement in community development has tended to be cyclical and criticism of it has been intense. Its adversaries have suggested that the enthusiasm of the proponents of community development has outweighed sound judgment as to what programs were, in fact, worthwhile (Petersen & Petersen 1960). Indeed, since the goals of community development projects are often broad and vaguely defined, their outcomes may defy measurement. The ultimate test of effectiveness would seem to lie in the consequence of community decisions taken and of this, there is little concrete evidence.

There appears little agreement as to the propriety of university involvement in community development. Academics may characterize it as work not of "university level" or as an enterprise which does not involve research of reputable quality. Indeed, some regard it not as education at all but rather as a kind of social agitation. Among its most bitter critics are businessmen who argue that when the university becomes emeshed in the controversy surrounding a community issue, it loses its reputation for objectivity, its independence of thought, and the integrity of its credentials as a neutral (Gaynor 1974). Certainly, the institution's politicization is a clear danger. Other hazards include the possibility that a kind of low-grade social welfare may be substituted for the university's unique function, education, or that the university-based community development project may be infiltrated by external vested interests.

The criteria which ought properly to govern university engagement in community development seem clear. Involvement in it must be characterized by professional and ethical performance of the highest order. The research related to community problems must demonstrate a competent methodology, strict avoidance of manipulation of individuals or groups, and the existence of clearly definable, achievable and socially defensible goals. The choice of constituency to be served must be that of the institution and the problem to be solved appropriate to institutional resources.

Community Services

Almost from their inception, the universities of North America and particularly the land-grant institutions of the United States have offered cultural opportunities to the whole community and have been the focal point of its aesthetic development. Canadian institutions followed suit. In 1908, the President of the new University of Alberta, for example, proclaimed "that the extension of the activities of the university on such lines as will make its benefits reach directly and indirectly the mass of the people, carrying its ideals of refinement and culture into their minds and its latent spiritual and moral power into their minds and hearts, is a work second to none" (Corbett 1954, 100–1). If ordinary people, Henry Marshall Tory argued, were to hear concerts, participate in theater, see exhibitions of paintings and have access to books in the Alberta of that day, it would only be because the University undertook to provide them the opportunity.

Across North America, university services are today extraordinarily diverse and, while only indistinctly related to education, are nonetheless significant. They include lecture series, concerts plays, public debates, the circulation of films and audiovisual equipment, speakers' bureaus, demonstrations in home economics and agriculture, or the printing of helpful publications. Indeed, it is difficult to imagine a modern society without access to such opportunities.

But times and circumstances have changed. The university is no longer the only institution in the community able to extend cultural resources. In fact, the current question is what services reasonably ought to be continued. In terms of the expenditure of funds and effort involved, the university's public service activities might be classified in three ways. There are those in which the public is merely given access to an existing facility of the university—its galleries or arboreta and occasionally its libraries. Other services organized by the university, and often directed to particular publics, include special events such as concerts, recitals, special lecture series; the university press which may undertake to publish the work not only of its own scholars but of others in the community; and television programs which are prepared for a community audience. A third category of university public service activity is the intense use by the community of university facilities and staff for consultation or research or training or the provision of learning materials.

Which of its service activities the university will wish to sustain will depend on the extent and intensity of its relationship with the constituency it serves. Certain guiding criteria are apparent. The activities should be of university level, however each institution may define that slippery concept. The university should not compete with other agencies or undertake what commercial firms do for profit. A key consideration is the extent to which the community services of the institution should pay their way. Influencing all of this is the university's judgment of what community interest, what clientele and what geographic segment of its constituency it should attempt to serve. A related question is whether the university should regard the separate efforts of its departments and faculties as its collective contribution to the community or whether, through centralization, it should rigorously select and define that limited group of services in which it will concentrate its energy.

Part-time credit studies which in their presentation are merely an extension of the institution's conventional program may not adequately meet adult needs. A review of university provision of part-time credit studies might appropriately consider such issues as these: Who are the adult students thus to be served? What are their learning needs and, thus, what adaptations of conventional course content ought to be made? How can the institution modify its present administrative procedures the better to serve adults?

Continuing professional education, now appropriately described as a growth industry, is the largest part of continuing education. Certainly, the professional must keep abreast of the rapid advance of modern technology; but, since he practices in a world quite different from that in which he was trained, he ought also to have a knowledge of the character and values of that changed society. The prudent university ought to give careful attention not only to practices in the provision of continuing professional education but also to significant issues and vested interests, its own included, in this exploding segment of education.

Once the core of continuing education programs, noncredit liberal studies today play a minor role. Yet to adult learners seeking to enrich their lives or preparing for change in career, their educational potential is large. Not guided by an underlying philosophy, this part of university continuing education program consists largely of unrelated fragments some of which, indeed, are clearly peripheral to the proper concern of a university. Nor does the noncredit liberal studies program exhibit that innovation which characterizes continuing education in vocational subjects.

While it is not usually a large element of university continuing education, the potential of community development to affect the university, positively or negatively, is large. The university's choice is plain: whether to confine its connection with the community to that of educator and critic or whether to assume a responsibility as a shaper of society, as a body which identifies social wrongs and leads in righting them. The implicit danger to the university engaging in community development is that its involvement may corrode institutional objectivity. But through stipulating the criteria which are to govern university intervention in the affairs of the community, that hazard can be lessened.

Only by the most elastic definition can the array of community services provided by the university be labelled "continuing education." Yet their provision is expected by the community and parts of such service may well be a responsibility of the institution's continuing education division. In the interests of efficiency and effectiveness, the extent and intensity of such services to the community should be guided by appropriate criteria.

University continuing education program has grown haphazardly through *ad hoc* responses to a variety of pressures and strongly influenced by the enrollment economy usually imposed on the function and, indeed, if university continuing education program is to be effective in its service to the community it must remain flexible and adaptable. Yet, if that program is to serve the goals of the university, its choice must be guided by criteria which reflect the institution's ideals. What necessarily precedes the establishment of those criteria are answers to these questions: Whom is the university to serve? What are their real needs? What resources of the university can be deployed to meet those needs? How best might these resources be applied?

4   The Design and Delivery of University Continuing Education

A variety of factors influence both the design of continuing education programs and how they are presented to the consumer—the adult learner. The intention here is to set out basic concepts underlying current practice in program design, to explore how programs are conceived and developed, and to examine issues in the delivery of these programs.

The Bases of Continuing Education Design

The adult learner differs significantly from traditional students in his attitudes, expectations and requirements. He aspires to be self-directing; past experience and occupation will influence what he wishes to learn; he is resistant to a pattern willed on him by the institution; he prefers action-oriented learning techniques to the lecture mode. Moreover, and this fact is important, he is not only willing to be involved in the planning of his learning experience but *expects* to be involved (Knowles 1969). The University of California, Berkeley, which annually enrolls some 50,000 adult learners describes them thus:

They are more rewarding, more challenging, and more critical than undergraduate students. . . . The adult student, not pursuing a degree—and most of them do not—is eclectic in the humanities, interested . . . in specific aspects of a subject but not usually in its totality, interested in limited sequences of courses [and different from] the graduate student of the humanities who although he may have a passionate thirst for knowledge, is really apprenticed to a learned trade in the humanities. . . . The passionate pilgrims among adult students are just about as frequent as among the younger . . . [but] it is the rare adult who will submit himself or herself eagerly to the typical disciplinary approach of humanities subject matter. The adult student is an interdisciplinary animal by nature . . . and it is of utmost importance to understand this in programming and teaching (Stern 1979, 2–5).

Such assumptions about adult learners which guide much of practice in university continuing education connect to issues common to all of postsecondary education: the nature of teaching and learning; the relationship of inquiry to teaching; the connection between the discipline and its application; the relationship of instructor to student; and the balance between instructor input and student initiative (Beck 1977). They can be integrated as a model.*

Program

Adult learners perceive themselves as different from regular day-time students and expect to be treated as autonomous individuals.

Adult learners seek education to achieve specific, identifiable goals. Their reasons for enrolling include intellectual growth and social contact.

Adult learners want education which is related to job or life situations. Their approach to education is problem-centered; they tend to be more interested in the application of knowledge than in theory.

Their attendance in courses and programs can not always be continuous. Adult learners desire to complete their educational objectives with the minimum time expenditure.

---

*Adapted from Robert W. Comfort, "Higher Adult Education Programming: A Model," *Adult Leadership*, vol. 23, no. 1 (1974), pp. 6–32.

Instruction

Adult learners enter a program with a high readiness to learn.
Adult students can learn and achieve as well as regular day-time students.
The motivation of the adult to learn will vary throughout his educational experience.
Experience outside the classroom can be harnessed to the reinforcement of learning.
Adult learning appropriately begins at a point which connects to his concerns.
Certain factors may retard the adult's ability to learn: a pre-disposition to react in patterned ways; emotional associations; self-image; lack of study skills. To optimize learning, adults require freedom.

Admission

Admissions should be based upon assessment of ability to achieve a predetermined level.
A high probability exists that the adult may not complete degree requirements.
Adults will periodically discontinue and return to educational programs.
Nonclassroom learning may equate to classroom content.

Counselling

Learning problems result from such characteristics as these: emotional associations, patterns of thought, time availability, orientation to learning, role and self-concept.
Learning problems may stem from the whole of the adult's life situation including family and job.
Counselling maximizes the probability of learner goal completion.

These are typical characteristics of the adult learner which one might expect to see recognized in typical formats of university continuing education programs which are characterized in Figure 1.

FIGURE 1

Typical Formats of University Continuing Education Programs

CONFERENCE: A general type of meeting usually of one or more days' duration, attended by a fairly large number of people. A conference will have a central theme but is often loosely structured to cover a wide range of topics. The emphasis is on prepared presentations by authoritative speakers, although division into small group sessions for discussion purposes is often a related activity.

INSTITUTE: Generally similar to a conference, but more tightly structured to provide a more systematic development of its theme, with the emphasis more on providing instruction in principles and techniques than on general information. Participants are usually individuals who already have some competence in the field of interest. Institute programs may have a certain continuity, meeting on a yearly basis for example.

SHORT COURSE: A sequential offering, as a rule under a single instructor, meeting on a regular basis for a stipulated number of class sessions over a short period of time (e.g., one to three weeks, etc.). Quizzes and examinations may be given depending upon the determination of requirements. The noncredit course . . . may resemble the credit course in everything but the awarding of credit. It may also be more informal and more flexible in its approach in order to meet the needs of students.

WORKSHOP: Usually meets for a continuous period of time over a period of one or more days. The distinguishing feature of the workshop is that it combines instruction with laboratory or experiential activity for the participants. The emphasis is more likely to be on skill training than on general principles.

SEMINAR: A small grouping of people with the primary emphasis on discussion under a leader or resource person or persons. In continuing higher education a seminar is more likely to be a one-time offering, although it may continue for several days.

SPECIAL TRAINING PROGRAM: A skill program which offers a combination of instruction and practice. The approach is usually on a more individualized basis than a workshop.

Source: Commission on Colleges, Southern Association of Colleges and Schools, *The Continuing Education Unit: Guidelines and Other Information* (Atlanta: 1973), Appendix A, p. 15.

The components of these formats and the decision points encountered in framing each are capsulized in Figure 2.

FIGURE 2

Decision Points and Components of a Continuing Education Program

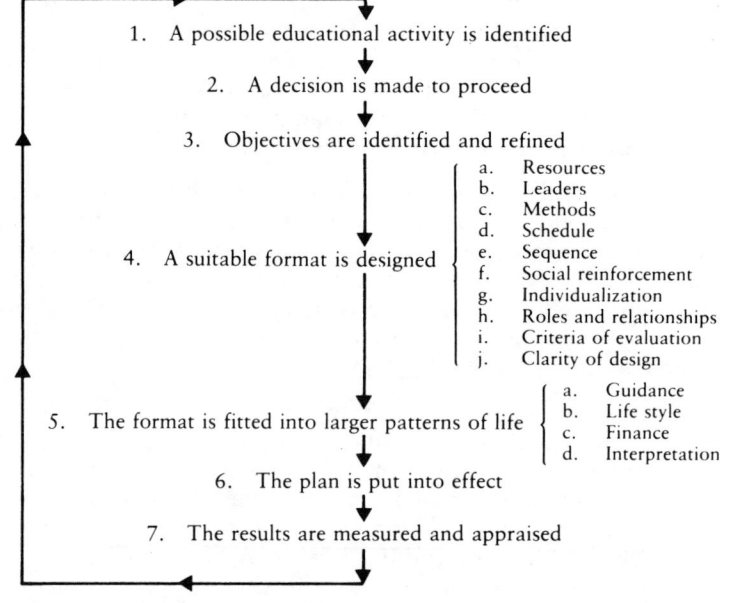

1. A possible educational activity is identified
2. A decision is made to proceed
3. Objectives are identified and refined
4. A suitable format is designed
   - a. Resources
   - b. Leaders
   - c. Methods
   - d. Schedule
   - e. Sequence
   - f. Social reinforcement
   - g. Individualization
   - h. Roles and relationships
   - i. Criteria of evaluation
   - j. Clarity of design
5. The format is fitted into larger patterns of life
   - a. Guidance
   - b. Life style
   - c. Finance
   - d. Interpretation
6. The plan is put into effect
7. The results are measured and appraised

Source: Cyril O. Houle, *The Design of Education* (San Francisco: Jossey-Bass, 1972), p.47. Reprinted by permission of the publisher.

Program Choice and Development

How curriculum ought to be chosen and how most effectively to develop it are key questions which would seem to demand answers from processes more sophisticated than intuition.* The justification of university continuing education, one supposes, and the realization through it of institutional purposes should begin with an accurate identification of the educational needs of the adult community, a review of what institutional resources can be employed in meeting them, a decision as to what response by the university institution might be most appropriate (a judgment best made against pre-established criteria).

---

*The dozen processes employed in the order in which they are most frequently used is set out in Nathan C. Shaw, ed., *Administration of Continuing Education* (Washington, D.C.: National Association for Public School Adult Education, 1969), p. 171.

In fact, a 1978 U.S. study concludes that university continuing education program is largely initiated by the continuing education staff on an *ad hoc* basis (Durnall 1978). In reality, much of program in university continuing education is a product of "opportunistic surveillance" rather than of research-based planning incorporating community participation. But, as a British educator puts it, "programs for adults . . . should not be the spontaneous, slapdash outgrowth of deliberations by a single armchair academician whose understanding of the psychological and sociological factors which influence the curriculum development process is either consciously or unconsciously impoverished" (Lumsden 1977, 279–80). Moreover, as Lewis Mumford on observing the same principle in a not unconnected field puts it, "It is naive to think [specialists] can by themselves formulate social needs and purposes that underlie a good . . . plan: the work of the philosopher, the educator, the artist, the common man is no less essential; and unless they are brought into the process of planning, as both critics and creators, the values that will be imported into the plan, when it is finally made, will be merely those that have been carried over from past situations and past needs, without critical revision: old dominants, not fresh emergents" (as quoted in Lumsden 1977, 280–81). The expanding clientele of adult learners may well find unacceptable the kind of educational components or building blocks in which the university normally deals and note the absence of thoughtful and sensitive planning by the institution. Further, the education needs of business, professional and other groups are pluralistic and they can only be met by a pluralistic response from an institution which must also be prepared to adapt quickly to shifts in market demand (National Advisory Council on Extension and Continuing Education 1975).

Clearly, since such education must be flexible, adaptable and reflect adult needs, it would seem prudent that the university establish in advance those criteria which are intended to guide its choice of continuing education program. A comprehensive set of objectives for adult education generally and a strategy for achieving them is, in fact, provided by UNESCO (n.d.); but because they are broad and even platitudinous, they provide at best only a general guide to university continuing education. Closer to the mark is a set of guidelines developed by Whale (1972) which identifies a suitable program which encourages the adult to learn how to learn, which provides counselling about educational objectives, which gives emphasis to skills in communication and decision-making, which provides a wide enough range of subject matter in a variety of forms, which gives attention to the social aspects of the learning process, and which offers to learners the opportunity of testing their learning in practice sessions in the relative security of the classroom before applying it in the outside world.

What continuing education program is chosen will clearly be affected by a judgment — perhaps more likely to be that of individuals than of the institution itself — as to whom the university is to serve. What recent data confirm is that the university's continuing education constitutency is today predominantly middle-class. Other elements of society may be inadequately served or remain unserved. Among those who may be educationally disadvantaged are older people, or women (whose role has changed categorically in a generation) or would-be learners remote from the campus. Historically, much of change in higher education has been generated by pressures from outside of the academy. Today, among those external pressures is the relentless sweep towards an egalitarian social philosophy, constantly escalating costs and the anxious groping of citizens for ways to preserve individual identities against the stultifying machinery of contemporary civilization. These inter-related pressures — which have been labeled the access problem, the finance problem and the goal problem — are key influences in the conduct of continuing education and, indeed, on higher education generally (Vermilye 1974).

Inevitably, the objectivity of whomever chooses and executes the program will be questioned simply because of the value judgments implicit in it. But value judgments are unavoidable and inherent in the design of the continuing education program, in the choice of instructional staff, in the selection of students and in the instructional process itself which, too, will incorporate the beliefs of the instructor (Fordham 1975; Wiltshire 1972; James 1971; Andragogues 1974; Jessup 1977; and Jones 1971). But recognition of this circumstance and the postulation of criteria to govern program choices at least would abate the more gross offences against objectivity.

A related problem is that of determining what is to comprise "university level" standard in continuing education. With respect to credit courses, there is within each university the machinery for determining what level is appropriate. But in contrast, the advance review of noncredit continuing education programs by university councils is rare. Indeed, a considerable proportion of university continuing education programs—many of them in management subjects—are designed, directed and in all significant ways, their instruction included, controlled by organizations which are external to the university. In this circumstance, clearly, the university has little opportunity to judge how consistent in their intellectual content such programs may be with institutional goals. The external agency becomes the educative force and the university merely the purveying mechanism. Nonetheless, the public will almost certainly construe such programs as reflective of the ideals of the university. The image and standards of the university, in short, are reflected in considerable part not only through its conventional offerings of credit courses but as well through its continuing education program.

One of the remarkable features of adult education in Canada in the last two decades has been the creation of agencies in business, government, agriculture, labor, service organizations and professional organizations to provide education and training to adult learners. Where, relatively few years ago, the university was the principal and in some instances the only institutional provider of continuing education, there now exists a host of agencies which include a much expanded network of community colleges and technical institutions which are able to serve and actively intend to expand their service to the community. This suggests that the university, a unique pool of resources, ought to undertake only that continuing education program which it can do best and quite deliberately leave the remainder to other agencies. The periodic review and pruning of its continuing education program in consultation particularly with the colleges and technical institutes would help the university institution to achieve a character in its own program consistent with its unique goals.

Many criticisms of university continuing education program center on its coherence. Adult students argue that the credit courses comprised in it represent only insubstantial fragments of the whole curriculum of the institution rather than carefully scheduled elements of linked patterns of offerings such as would efficiently enable students to achieve their educational goals. A frequent complaint is that university subject departments do not make themselves sufficiently responsible for the content of courses offered under off-campus auspices. The charge is made that the off-campus program of credit courses is often narrowly constructed, largely in service to school teachers. Frustration is expressed at seeming university resistance to the integration of credit and noncredit work and exasperation is voiced at the seeming ambivalence of inter-institutional transfer policies. Accompanying these expressions of discontent is an assortment of others: that the tuition fees demanded seek to recover a much larger share of costs than is expected from full-time students; that it is often impossible to complete an undergraduate program without full-time residency; that the university encourages social inequality by neglecting to provide educational opportunities to persons at all social and economic levels (University of Saskatchewan 1973); and that university certificates, the status of which varies among institutions, are an unstable currency.

An important, earlier noted influence on the selection of continuing education program is the enrollment economy typically imposed by the university (Clark 1956). There is not infrequently pressure on the university's continuing education agency to provide institutional administrators with enrollment statistics sufficiently impressive to justify the continuance of the function. The predictable consequence of these and other pressures is the choice of programs by the continuing education division out of reasons which have less to do with the relevance of these programs to the goals of the institution and more with their capacity to generate revenue. Such necessity is the mother of strange bedfellows.

On and off the campus, there is nagging unease that the university continuing education program ranges over too wide an area and engages in subjects which are insignificant and peripheral to institutional goals. One critic, indeed, characterizes contemporary university continuing education as displaying untempered enthusiasm for faddism, for the transient in subject matter with its consequences in academic shoddiness. The advertised claims for these programs which may persuade the student that he will get something for nothing lead only to his disillusionment. The very title of his critique, "The Thrills and Shills of Lifelong Learning," suggests what faculty and public may suspect: the negative influence of marketplace hyperbole on the institution's continuing education program. The warning is emphatic if vulgar: "We live in a world of hype [and need] to keep our crap detectors charged" (DeMott 1978, 55).

This is stringent criticism indeed. Acceptance of it and recognition of the need for universities to provide a new policy framework for continuing education has prompted a series of recommendations by a group of leading figures in higher education in a Kellogg Foundation study. "All university lifelong education programs must be of the highest quality . . . quality should be continually monitored . . . To determine the extent to which various lifelong education experiences serve long-term needs, time-lapse surveys should be conducted . . . The university should . . . ensure the employment of a greater percentage of faculty familiar with, concerned about, and capable of lifelong educational activity. Criteria for salary increases, promotions and academic grants, and awarding of tenure should reflect the lifelong education contributions of faculty members. The tuition for courses should be equal on and off campus. Whenever possible, continuing education activities should be assigned to faculty members as part of regularly compensated duties" (Hesburgh, Miller & Wharton 1973, 105–10).

Clearly, the implementation of such remedies requires the will of the university's councils to accept responsibility for the quality of the continuing education program, for the adequate counselling of students and for the revision of a funding base which is at the root of many of its problems. From the expansion of the last two decades, university continuing education must shift to innovation and the attainment of quality (Munroe 1973, 48).

Despite this catalogue of problems real enough as they are, it would be a lopsided judgment which did not acknowledge the occasionally energetic, often ingenious and certainly extensive response of the university to its adult constituency. The importance of this growing clientele to the institution is indisputable. What have been identified are issues in program choice and development which the university must recognize and solve if it is better to serve adult learners, and in so doing, to serve itself.

Counselling the Adult Learner

A recurring complaint of the adult returning to the campus to supplement his education is the clumsy fashion in which he is received.

The political reality (which it would be prudent for the university to acknowledge) is that these adult students are tax-paying citizens and that their credentials, when thoughtfully examined, may well be as sound as those of their youthful counterparts. In addition, they may carry job and family responsibilities not borne by the younger student: they may be working forty to fifty hours a week, sometimes at unsocial hours; they may have small children who need care; they may be burdened with personal and financial worries (Kegel 1977). Thus, in returning to education, they may need special encouragement.

To aid this significant segment of the student body would not be difficult. A starting point is for the university to persuade itself—in its own interests—that the adult student ought to be helped at least as much as his counterpart in the conventional student body. Most useful would be the inclusion in the institutional calendar of a section addressing the particular concerns of the adult student, and provision of special brochures and posters giving information on the educational, financial and social services available to him on and off campus. The scheduling of registration at times convenient to the working adult and the use of locations off-campus would be advantageous as would orientation programs, designed specifically to explain to adult students the services on which they might draw.

Perhaps most important, adult students ought to have access to expert counselling. Many of them have been away from formal education for some time; in returning to it, not only may they doubt their own abilities but they may be intimidated by the cool impersonality of the institution. Counselling, a Carnegie report concludes, is the key to reaching a virtually untouched market of adult students (*Carnegie Quarterly* 1977).* What most adults urgently need as they come into continuing education are answers to such questions as these: What steps should I take to improve my life or expand my career? What training or education do I need? From what sources is it available? How can I get started? These and like questions are at the root of a new thrust in the United States:

---

*But University of British Columbia's Myrne Nevison in a December 5, 1983 conversation warns that inept and inexperienced counsellors (and most of them are ill-trained), are dangerous; indeed no counsellor is better than an untrained one (*Canadian Magazine* 1979, 2).

educational brokering.* Educational brokers are go-betweens, mediators between adult learners and the complex array of adult education opportunities. They serve through giving information, through referral, through counselling and through client advocacy. The process of matching learner needs and interests to appropriate learning resources is a crucial one to the learning society (Cross 1978, 39).

Instructional Technology

With the invention of the printing press in 1453, the universities of Europe recognized that the days of the vellum manuscript were numbered. Over succeeding centuries, they established themselves as producers of intellectual, religious and political books. But universities have been less responsive to broadcasting as a medium for disseminating knowledge. The academic world has, in general, failed to make use of the new media to communicate with the public at large and has also neglected to use it effectively within the university itself (MacCormack 1975). In fact, it is only recently that the impact of television in education has been examined and despite the growth of other technologies, television remains a most significant vehicle for education. Of the potential of instructional technology generally, not enough is known about the effects of electronic media on the individual or about how instant communication, total information retrieval and the other products of advanced technology can best fit into the design of a teaching institution. What is alleged, however, is that present instructional forms are so archaic that their purposes, functions and practices seem hardly to fit this modern age (Cohen 1969, xix).

Certainly the best known, most successful and most widely imitated application of instructional technology is Great Britain's Open University to which Smith (1975, 173) attributes these advantages. The system can bring high quality learning material to

---

*For additional information about this new service to adult learners and its extent in the United States, see the Bulletin of the National Center for Education Brokering, 405 Oak Street, Syracus, N.Y. 13203.

the individual in his own home or in a local study center or college. It avoids the high capital cost associated with establishing a conventional residential university and can deploy a relatively small body of academic staff to provide courses for very large numbers of students. Able to provide an ongoing system of continuing education to adults it can also deliver a wide range of carefully devised and evaluated learning materials to other parts of the postsecondary education system. With appropriate modifications and more flexibility in the interchange of credits, it could be used in association with a range of institutions of higher education, to provide a wider spectrum of opportunity at higher level.

But the assumption that, because it has been functional and successful in Britain, educational television might readily be replicated elsewhere is unwarranted. Such an assumption fails to take into account the very considerable differences between the U.K. and other countries: geographic differences, differences in the characteristics of national communication systems, differences in the number of university places available in each society and differences in the pattern of population distribution. Moreover, and the point is sometimes missed, in the Open University the television medium is, in fact, subordinate to more traditional methods of study; the basic tools remain those of reading and writing.

Excepting two well-established developments in Canada, television as an educational medium has not flourished in North America, in part perhaps, because of misunderstandings about the medium itself and in part because of the complexity of the problems associated with educational programming (Parkin 1975). Although broadcast can leap distance barriers, it can do so with only one message at a time, or with as many messages as there are channels. Since much of continuing education is offered in the evenings, the educator is obliged to compete with commercial interests seeking the largest audiences of the day. In the airtime likely to be available, only a very small number of subjects can be tackled. Yet adults are interested not only in a very wide range of subjects but in varying levels within that range. Student dislike of the dehumanizing aspect of the technology which makes possible educational television and other novel delivery systems has certainly been a factor constraining application of the medium: the loss of face-to-face contact with the instructor is an especially inhibiting factor of the greatest importance (MacCormack 1975; Parkin 1975; and Sapper 1975).

If students have resisted courses which employ the media, faculty have as well. Faculty aversion to the employment of materials and equipment associated with television is often vigorous. Because teaching is a personal, highly individual art, those faculty members using the media have tended to insist on being closely engaged in the creation of their own materials, a determination which may well have hindered program development. The production of first-rate materials, even such simple devices as slides and transparencies, require good quality equipment and expert assistance which are not always available. The student consumer, accustomed to the expertly crafted products of commercial television, will not find the unsophisticated efforts of the amateur acceptable. This reality is often overlooked: that the materials employed in educational television must be of a technical standard competitive with the glossy commercial product which sets the standard of technical excellence. To create effective yet competitive programs is costly and that cost is frequently underestimated. Finally, its enthusiasts have occasionally over-estimated the potential of educational technology which has prompted sometimes absurd claims: "Crippled and want to take university courses . . . Turn to your terminal and learn all about electronics (or whatever) through querying and responding to questions appearing on the screen" (*Financial Post* 1978).

For such reasons, the media in education have not realized the promise which they held out a decade ago. Indeed, "the present status of instructional technology in American education is low in both quantity and quality. Rather than taking hold and gaining followers through successful demonstrations, many ambitious projects have faltered and failed. Rather than boldly exploring fresh strategies to stimulate learning, most projects have merely translated existing curricula and teaching into the newer media. Rather than filling a functional role in a comprehensive approach to the design of instruction, most users have chosen or been forced to confine themselves to their own special medium or technique. Rather than moving into the center of the planning process in education, most technologically oriented educators are on the periphery" (Meierhenry 1977, 13).

On the positive side, educational technology has without question stimulated tangential but encouraging developments. Evident is a revived interest in the individualization of instruction, amply described in the literature and now common in practice. Another is the creation, relatively recently in North America, of university offices responsible for the improvement of instruction. There are attempts at joint teacher-student action to improve instruction. Promotion and tenure recommendations (in which students may have a voice) appear to give greater attention to the quality of teaching (Meierhenry 1977). The General Secretary of Britain's Association of University Teachers suggests this substantial benefit of the Open University: that it has produced a new kind of academic staff member, flexible in his approach towards his subject, conversant with the rationale of television media and, of necessity, inventive in ways of putting his material over to students. All of which is a leavening that does much to broaden the scope and outlook of the profession as a whole (Sapper 1975).

In Canada, two examples of the sustained and coherent application of technology to higher education are the programs of Quebec's Télé-Université and Alberta's Athabasca University. The former services about 20,000 students in distance education programs, offering courses which are essentially multi-media packages used in conjunction with regional group meetings (Daniel & Umbriaco 1975). Athabasca University enrolls about 9,000 students in distance education programs, towards the Bachelor of Arts, Bachelor of General Studies and Bachelor of Administration degrees, through courses that are self-paced, multi-media packages, accompanied by strong emphasis on counselling, credit coordination and career planning (Athabasca University 1979). Rather more recent and serving 3,000 learners in British Columbia's vast hinterland is the Open Learning Institute which offers instruction towards the Bachelor of Arts and Bachelor of Arts in Administrative Studies, career and technical courses for provincially recognized certificates and distance learning opportunities in adult basic education.

Since an expansion in the use of technology for education seems certain, what can be distilled out of experience with educational television which can offer sensible guidance? Broadcast serves better for purposes of enrichment than as a total instructional package. If credit courses are to be offered, correspondence work should be the core, supplemented by radio and television, and not the other way around. Full control of the preparation of the program should be lodged exclusively neither with the producers nor with the teachers, however experienced, sophisticated or brilliant they may be; a working partnership is critical to success. In many topics, learning does not suffer when radio is substituted for television, and radio is very much less expensive. Costs in the preparation and distribution of educational programs are breathtakingly high; inter-institutional cooperation in the development of educational networks, in the exchange of tapes, in the development of courses is essential. Adult students, many of whom are employed, have trouble fitting one-time broadcasts into their schedules. Programs can, of course, be re-broadcast; but the long run effectiveness of radio and television in education programs depends on the availability of audio and video tapes at scattered locations, on short notice, and at convenient times (Harrington 1977, 78–79).

Accreditation: The Continuing Education Unit

Ours has been termed a credential-oriented society. Appropriate credentials are vital to the job seeker and it is no surprise that an American study (Carp, Peterson & Roelfs 1974) indicates that two-thirds of would-be learners wish to receive some form of recognition for their efforts, while the Waniewicz study (1976) of such preferences in Ontario determined that nearly 70 percent of adult learners wish to achieve a degree or diploma.

The assignment of credit to individual university courses and their accumulation towards a degree is today the single best-established feature of higher education in North America. Its roots lie in the influence of German universities on the development of North American graduate schools which led to the formation of academic departments, stimulated curricula diversification, the invention of course credits and, necessarily, a procedure to record them. So entrenched is the system that it is difficult today to imagine an alternative (Warren 1974).

The significance of credit increases as an expanding volume of students, intent on broadening their mix of learning withdraw from and subsequently re-enter an institution or transfer from one institution to another. Credits serve as a kind of token or symbol both to the individual student and to the world at large of progress towards a goal. Credits influence students to channel their efforts in an orderly fashion down disciplinary paths. The record of their accumulation may be requisite to an application for a job or for admission to a professional school or for an occupational license.

In recent years, there has been created a demand for the recognition of educational accomplishments achieved independently of degree course studies. To those who argue that forms of learning external to conventional education—previous employment, independent study, travel, supervised study—cannot be properly assessed, an increasingly frequent response is that they can, in fact, be validated through standardized examinations. In any event, it is argued, the inadequacies within the present credit system are great: grades may vary with student performance while credits do not; the number of credits may not reflect the student's level of performance; standards in examinations vary and there is disagreement among instructors as to what constitutes satisfactory performance (Open University Committee on Continuing Education 1976). In assessing nontraditional study, the university is typically inclined to caution for good reasons. The assessor may be isolated from the learning situation or unfamiliar with it. The possibility of fraud or error or overstatement exists. There may be uncertainty as to what learning was attempted by the student, how it proceeded and how it concluded. Yet, increasingly, competence in academic areas acquired other than through traditional courses is being determined through the use of standardized tests such as those of the College Level Exam Program (CLEP) (Warren 1974).

Prior to the turn of the century, postsecondary education provided a narrow, substantially homogeneous set of experiences directed towards a limited range of goals. Today, post-secondary education includes an extraordinary range of programs, options within many of them diverse, and thus an almost infinitely broad spectrum of goals. The very multiformity of programs suggests that there should also be a parallel diversity of assessment measures, of validating processes, of certificates of performance. A Carnegie Commission report proposes that short programs with specific goals have as legitimate a claim to formal academic recognition as any two-year or four-year degree program (Warren 1974, 137). The prediction is that the undergraduate degree can no longer be the sole endpoint in education: that the combined strains of increasingly complex technology requiring highly developed skills, and political pressures for social and economic equality are not likely to permit the four-year degree permanently to remain a dominant terminal point in higher education. Instead, a variety of formal terminal points may develop which mark departure points for job entrance, for licensing or certification or for further education to be undertaken later. This greater diversity of terminal points would require a more elaborate definition of credits than that now existing (Warren 1974, 144–145).

A mechanism devised to record the unconventional learning experiences of adults is the "Continuing Education Unit," described as including "all institutional and organizational learning experiences in organized formats that impart noncredit education to postsecondary level learners" (Donnelly n.d.) and defined as "ten contact hours of participation in an organized continuing education experience under responsible sponsorship, capable direction and qualified instruction" (National Task Force on the Continuing Education Unit 1974, 31). Its objectives are these:

- the systematizing, recording and reporting of participation in noncredit continuing education
- the provision of a uniform system for accumulating statistical data on participation in continuing education
- the labelling of this data as it accumulates and its transfer to the continuing education record of the individual
- the encouragement of the long-range educational goals of the student and his pursuit of knowledge for personal or professional purposes.

The goals are clear enough and the mechanics of instituting the continuing education unit appear difficult but not insuperable.*

---

*How the CEU might be employed is set out in *The Continuing Education Unit: Guidelines and other information*, prepared by the Commission on Colleges of the Southern Association of Colleges and Schools (Atlanta, Georgia, 1973); in *The Continuing Education Unit: Criteria and Guidelines*, prepared by The National Task Force on the Continuing Education Unit (Washington, D.C.: NUEA, 1979); in *The Continuing Education Unit* by Anne C. Kaplan and Clive C. Veri, ERIC Report 94213 (Washington, D.C.: Education Resources Information Center, 1974); in *The Continuing Education Unit* (Washington, D.C.: National Task Force on the Continuing Education Units, 1970); and in *Handbook of Criteria and Procedures for Continuing Education Unit Programs* (East Lansing, Mich.: Continuing Education Service, Michigan State University, 1977).

According to a 1976 U.S. Department of Health, Education and Welfare report, somewhat more than a third of American colleges and universities now use this device to report continuing education activities. This figure, the more startling because the continuing education unit is a new device, is one of which prudent institutions might well take note (National Center for Education Statistics 1978b), but with caution. What its opponents chiefly fear, and with cause, is that the application of this device will surely degrade quality in education: that for sustained, searching inquiry into a subject will be substituted shallow, incoherent fragments of attention untouched by the intellect.

Yet it becomes increasingly difficult to argue that the conventional three-year degree has the only claim — or a more legitimate claim — to validity than do short programs with specific goals. Changing patterns in society are inevitably reflected in changing patterns of education if with some lag. The time is ripe for a wholesale review of the award of credit in both conventional and nontraditional education.

Innovative Practices in Continuing Education

Technological growth among other factors has made it impractical for the whole of education to be acquired between the ages of six and twenty-three; and thus, that it must progress intermittently over a lifetime. Concurrently, an increasingly assertive public is challenging many of the conventional assumptions of higher education: its direction, the residence requirement, the breadth of its purposes; and the acceptability of non-conventional learning.

Spurred by such challenges and also by a coincidental decline in their student body with consequently diminished budgets, North American institutions are experimenting with new approaches to the delivery of higher education. Over fifty such have been catalogued by Purdue University alone (Smith 1974) and as many more are detailed in a study undertaken by the Western Inter-State Commission for Higher Education (Barber 1975). Despite their seeming variety, however, these innovations can be grouped under a baker's dozen of headings:

LEARNING MODULES. Blocks of linked, learning segments so constructed that the learner can proceed in mastering them in the classroom or independently.
CREDIT FOR EXPERIENCE. The assessment of relevant life experiences which connect to what is being learned and their incorporation into a degree program or a continuing education unit.
PROFICIENCY EXAMINATION. Such examinations are used to determine the student's general level of achievement or his competence in particular subject areas. Widely in use in the United States is the College Proficiency Examination Program and the College Level Examination Programs.
SHORT TERM COURSES. Irregular programs of instruction in a wide variety of subjects which may incorporate travel or internships and which may or may not carry credit.
CONTINUING EDUCATION UNIT. The measurement of both formal and informal learning with a view to its subsequent recording in a "bank."
THE EXTERNAL DEGREE. Widely used internationally, the external degree is offered by an institution to distant learners. For many years, the University of London's external degree, for example, has been of immense practical advantage to the developing countries. It is usually based on a variety of learning experiences, formal and informal. Its proponents claim that exploration by the university of its feasibility sparks careful assessment of what is significant and what is ineffective in traditional higher educational processes.
CABLE TELEVISION. Implemented locally, regionally or nationally, this device offers the potential for study at home which may be supported by tutorial services or study group sessions or travelling library service.
CONTRACT LEARNING. The negotiation between student and teacher, in advance of instruction, of a mutually agreed content and level of performance required in a specific learning activity.
THE ADULT LEARNING PROJECT. This is a fresh approach to adult learning. Self-initiated, self-conducted, learning activities of adults are conducted outside of the framework of the institution though encouraged and supported by it.
CASSETTE INSTRUCTION. Audio and video cassettes today offer a wide range of learning materials. Related to them, and especially

useful in learning skills or techniques, are film loops. Available from a wide variety of sources, both are intended primarily for independent learning.

LEARNING VOUCHERS. Still little more than a notion, this concept centers on the idea of citizen entitlement to education, recognized by coupons or vouchers, which are surrendered to institutions which provide the education required at recurrent points in life.

PERIODIC ATTENDANCE. This concept involves institutional acceptance that the adult learner will himself determine the periods to be set aside for his education.

SELF-TRAINING WORKSHOPS. Instruction, often novel in character, combined with counselling, conducted to enable students to achieve personal growth through a variety of psychological experiences including therapy, analysis, meditation (Hiemstra 1977, 10–12).

Certain of these approaches have been well tested; the more active use of others lie in the future. Nor ought it to be supposed that any or all of these would be appropriate to every institution. What is critical is the willingness of institutions to entertain innovative practices. Such openness to innovation appears to be influenced by four factors. The availability of financial support specifically ear-marked for innovation will encourage the institution to innovate. What values predominate in the institution will affect the susceptibility to innovation; the more eminent it is, the less likely is the institution to move from conventional approaches. The intensity of competition among institutions critically influences the will to innovation. Finally, the more decentralized the decision-making structure, the more innovative is the institution likely to be (Clark 1968).

Something of practice in and attitudes towards innovation in North American institutions is reflected in a study of 1200 representative colleges and universities surveyed by a 1973 Commission on Non-Traditional Study (Ruyle and Geiselman 1974). Eighty-three percent of responding institutions, it is reported, actively encouraged adults over twenty-five to attend the university though the overwhelming majority of institutions expected these adult students to enroll in the conventional programs designed for youth. In three out of four of the institutions surveyed, the students were able to earn an undergraduate degree entirely by part-time attendance.

Generally, tuition rates appeared not to discriminate against part-time students who were eligible in more than one-half of the responding institutions for at least some kind of financial assistance. Most colleges and universities did not provide childcare facilities and in fewer than 10 percent of them were appropriate counselling services available. Only 4 percent of institutions encouraged intermittent study though half reported that, while they did not facilitate, they did not discourage it. Most institutions did not grant credit for work experience. At two-thirds of the institutions surveyed, it was possible for students to earn credit towards a degree or reduce the length of their program by scoring at an acceptable level on a recognized examination. Although most institutions were willing to grant credit by examination, at least 40 percent of those surveyed reported no real encouragement of students to earn credit by this means. The implementation of nontraditional learning opportunities for adults has not been without problems. Within the 1200 institutions surveyed, these eight of seventeen major obstacles encountered were the most common:

- lack of funds
- difficulty in assessing nonclassroom learning
- concern about academic standards
- faculty resistance
- budget based on FTE units
- lack of interest within the institution
- suspicion of the innovation as a passing fad
- lack of approved examination or other assessment techniques.

Evaluating the Product

Program evaluation, the process by which persons associated with an educational activity make judgments, based on evidence, about its effectiveness with the end in view of improving the educational activity is, of all the administrative tasks in continuing education that most complicated and difficult, least frequently attempted and often least rewarding (Knox 1974). Not unexpectedly, then, the quality of the continuing education output tends to be judged by the enrollment response to it: if a program is successful at the registration desk, it is good. Yet while there is some merit in such a judgment, this box-office criterion of success remains more apt to the theater than to the university.

The kinds of judgments fundamental to the evaluation process are those which compare expectations and performance. How close did the expected outcome of a program compare to its actual outcome? How well did the methodology employed by the instructor serve his adult students? Whether conducted formally or informally, evaluation is intended to monitor and diagnose an educational activity with a view to remedying its unsatisfactory aspects immediately or in the future. Structuring successful evaluation requires unequivocal answers to seven key questions. What specific purposes is it to serve? For whom is it intended? What features of the program are to be assessed? What evidence is to be collected? How is the evidence to be collected? How is it to be analysed? How is it to be reported (Groteleuschen 1979)?

Nothing could be of greater significance to the advance of the continuing education function — for that matter, to the whole of post secondary education function — than its implementation of valid processes for analysing its offerings so as to make possible the improvement of those which have merit and the elimination of others. Not only would this serve the objectives of the university, adult learners themselves would welcome an objective effort to measure both the content and the methodology in courses to which they have committed time, money and effort.

There is another broader face to evaluation. The estimated total of public investment in all levels of education for adults in the United States is said to exceed $3.5 billion annually (O'Keefe 1977), yet a general statement about the total benefits of that expenditure is impossible to make at present. Concrete evidence of the value to the nation of adult continuing education programs would be extraordinarily valuable.

About the future of continuing education, this can be predicted with assurance: that, as the level of their educational sophistication rises, adult learners will be more demanding of institutional competence in its provision. The sound design of continuing education program coupled to flexibility and imagination in its delivery become imperative. Prerequisite to this is an understanding of the attributes, attitudes and expectations of adults, a clientele of learners significantly different from youth, and a skillful reflection of these insights in program design and delivery.

Much of continuing education program is today a product of the random choice of perceived opportunities. A more suitable approach to the choice of program lies in the melding of a continuing survey of community interests to research-based planning, each to involve community input. Reasonably, the choice of program ought to conform to the goals of the institution as defined by pre-established criteria.

A serious criticism of university continuing education provision is its neglect of service to groups which might profit from the institution. In its continuing education provision, the university currently favors a middle-class clientele. With some reason, it has been charged with a lack of sympathy for and understanding of what has been termed "the wantlessness of the poor": the apathy of those who do not have enough education to know what elements of it they are capable of acquiring and using.

Other criticisms are made of university continuing education program: its low coherence; its frequent failure to meet and deal with normal constraints in the lives of adult learners; and inequity in its geographical provision. Some of it, offered under the banner of the university by organizations external to the campus, are not subject to inadequate control by the institution. Some of it, moreover, by any reasonable standard is inappropriate to the university institution.

The manner in which adults are received on the campus as they return to further their education is critical to the success of the university's continuing education efforts. The provision of expert counselling by the university is a means of reaching a large and hitherto untouched market of adult students. A contemporary, significant development is that of educational brokering services which through counselling, referral and advocacy connect adult students returning to learning with the most appropriate of the educational opportunities among the wealth of choices available. There is growing conviction that this is a potentially important device in closing gaps between adult learners and educational opportunities.

In North America, technology in general and television in particular is widely conceded to be a light that failed. Yet interest in its use in continuing education continues, very effectively in some few sources, and it seems to have spurred the improvement of instruction.

In this credential-oriented society, there is a rising demand from adult learners for recognition of their efforts whether in credit or noncredit programs or in a variety of learning experiences encountered elsewhere than on the campus. That this demand for recognition of their learning will increase seems likely. The use of the Continuing Education Unit, a device now increasingly employed to meet this need, has serious weaknesses.

A variety of innovative practices characterize postsecondary education in North America, some of them so recent that time has been insufficient to evalute them. A few of them might well be incorporated gradually into institutional practice.

Currently, there is renewed interest in the evaluation of the continuing education product which remains a difficult task. Reliable techniques of evaluation would be of considerable significance to institutional practice in continuing education as would indisputable evidence of the contribution of continuing education to the nation as a whole.

5   Organization and Policies

Two facts and an almost certain likelihood will influence the framework within which university continuing education is conducted and the policies which guide it. The first, evident from a variety of data, is rapidly advancing public participation in university continuing education. Continuing education has become much more visible; many more citizens are aware of its potential in their lives and look to the university to help them realize it. That is a challenge which, for good reasons, political and otherwise, the university would be unwise to ignore. Second, in recent years there has been an extraordinary expansion in the number and variety of institutional sponsors of continuing education, public and private. This fact inevitably prompts questions about the implications for the university about complementarity and competition. The likelihood is a decrease in the number of conventional students, those from eighteen to twenty-four years of age. Because of the effect of this reduction on budget of which about 80 percent flows to salaries, continuing education invites examination as a stabilizing element within the institution.

For the most part, the organization of continuing education on the campus has been the object of benign neglect. Its structure has not been the focus of the thoroughgoing discussion accorded to other institutional functions. Within the university itself, a variety of providers of adult learning opportunities have emerged—some of them complementary, some of them competitive with the institution's continuing education division. Continuing education divisions have been so busy responding to increasing public demand that few have had time to examine the implications of their growth or the underlying philosophy of the university in continuing education provision or the structure most appropriate to the task which, it is conceded, the heterogeneity of the adult student body makes the more difficult. The university's resources are not infinite. Clarifying the purpose of university continuing education is a prelude to contriving the structure best suited to administering it and would help assure that resources were deployed most productively in service to that purpose.

What follows is an examination of the function itself, its reflection in structure, the significant external relationships of the function, the role of government and policies in these matters: finance, staffing, marketing and research.

Function: The Basis of Structure

The framework from which university continuing education is offered in the North American university has changed as the function itself has expanded. Typically, the institution's few initial continuing education programs were conducted by its departments. The volume of courses having expanded, the function achieved organizational autonomy. Thus established, it has moved towards integration with the mainstream of the university to facilitate access to the whole of institutional resources and to achieve some measure of recognition and acceptance (Carey 1961). There is an alternative scenario: caught in a crossfire between public demand for its product and institutional expediency, the function may be integrated with the body of the university and disappear as a discrete unit.

In continuing education, as in the institution's other functions, an obvious first step in organization is the specification of goals. If the continuing education division is to achieve a sense of direction and an ideology or philosophy to which its staff can rally, if it is to build relationships which elicit external cooperation, and if it is to cultivate public understanding and support, then the university itself must establish for the division its goals in service to the adult learner. Agreement on the ends to be achieved at the institutional level ought clearly to precede the shaping of means at the divisional level.

The literature is replete with general statements on university role in continuing education. The University of Wisconsin expects the continuing education division to serve as a catalyst in the community, act as a bridge between the community and the university, develop liaison with other agencies in the field, stimulate and sometimes perform research, provide teaching and consulting services and, in short, make certain that the resources of the university at the division's disposal will be applied where they are most needed so as to benefit the whole of society (Harrington 1965, 36). The University of California specifies what continuing education ought *not* to be. It is *not* designed to recompense the university for the loss of full-time students due to attrition in conventional enrollment or to enhance the public relations image of the institution, or to fatten academic salaries, or to advance the careers of continuing educators. All these things are by-products of its primary goal: service to the people and the community (Frandson 1978b, 38).

From similar statements can be distilled the range of tasks of a university continuing education division:
- to monitor and coordinate continuing education programs and to assume budgetary responsibility for them
- to design, market and evaluate the worth of programs
- to provide, on and off the campus, a conspicuous focus of continuing education effort
- to act as a catalyst with others, on and off the campus, in achieving productive innovations in program; to establish and maintain liaison with the community for the purpose of meeting continuing education needs; and to conduct liaison with other agencies and institutions which provide continuing education with a view to achieving an efficient provision of education opportunities
- to manage technical and other services associated with the implementation of continuing education programs

- to acquire funds from private and governmental sources for programs, special projects and research
- to advance adult education as a field of study
- as requested, to provide overall policy direction in the achievement of an integrated and coordinated system of university continuing education provision (Hesburgh and others 1973, 95; Whale 1976; Selman 1973a).

To articulate the continuing education goals appropriate to an institution in a meaningful way, itself no small achievement, is only a preliminary step. As to the difficulty likely to be encountered in creating a revised structure for their accomplishment, Machiavelli's judgment is apt: "There is nothing more difficult to carry out, nor more doubtful of success, nor more dangerous to handle, than to initiate a new order of things. For the reformer has enemies in those who would profit by the old order, and only lukewarm defenders in all who would profit by the new order."

Structuring University Continuing Education

Certain general premises interconnect in the structuring of continuing education on the campus:
- The primary responsibility of university continuing education is the imparting of knowledge, skills and attitudes to adult learners who vary widely in their educational background.
- The education function should take precedence over the service role.
- Continuing education as a university function invites recognition parallel to that accorded teaching and research. (The corollary is that the level and quality of its programs must be such as to justify that recognition.)
- The basic instructional staff for university continuing education will be members of the university's regular academic staff; that instructional cadre will be supplemented by those from off the campus with special competencies.
- The design and presentation of university continuing education programs ought to reflect their continuing evaluation and new research findings.
- The university has a special responsibility to provide both opportunity for research into continuing education and training, at the graduate level, in that field.

- All of the elements of the continuing education thrust of the institution are best integrated or at least linked in some way.
- The organization of continuing education on the campus should include adequate mechanisms for consultation with the community (Kristjanson & Baker 1966).

The key characteristics of a continuing education division—the orientation intended for it, how formal its system, the number of levels of authority it comprises—provide a useful framework for the analysis of its structure. The orientation of the division may take any of four directions: towards function (task, job or method); towards subject matter (and especially whether learning content is disciplinary or interdisciplinary); towards its clientele (of adult learners); or towards territory, the geographic area it is intended to serve. To illustrate, a structure designed to emphasize *function* will focus on planning and matters related to administration. It will not ignore subject matter, clientele and territory but it will not emphasize them. (The summer session or correspondence study or distance education sections frequently follows this pattern). An approach to structural design which emphasizes *subject matter* will reflect either what are perceived to be the specific subject matter needs of adult learners or the professional orientation to disciplines typical within university departments—an important difference. The structure which emphasizes *clientele* will concern itself primarily with creating close relationships with particular publics or client groups: teachers, farmers, professionals, businessmen, women, the elderly or the alumni. Such a design emphasis may make provision to meet the needs of a particular clientele group for a particular kind of continuing education, or the need of the university itself to build mutual understanding and trust with that group. A *territorial* emphasis assumes a loyalty to, a predisposition to service of a particular geographic area, an approach which takes on obvious significance where other institutions provide service in a region.

The second feature in the organizational structure of university continuing education is the formality of its design and the degree to which that design is consciously planned and authorized. Formal structures encourage the assignment of roles and tasks, the evolvement of specialties and an improved capacity to accomplish objectives. But informal organizational design, that which is not authorized, not formally planned and neither tentative nor quite stable, may keep permanent roles and formal structural components to a minimum and thus afford the advantage of flexibility and the capacity to adapt quickly to new circumstances. Informal structures which continue tend to become part of the formal structure.

The third feature is the division's hierarchy: the number of distinct operating levels in its structure. Typically, the number of levels in university continuing education divisions is three or four: the dean or director, the professional programmers, the administrative assistants, and the clerical-secretarial staff. What is significant here is the level at which decisions are to be made and whether a flat or a pyramidal structure can most effectively combine administrative authority with the creative imagination of the specialist and the work of the support staff (Baker 1976; Gordon 1974).

A Kellogg Foundation report (Hesburgh, Miller & Wharton 1973) in a less analytical, more pragmatic approach to the design of university continuing education program observes that many of the administrative procedures on the campus have evolved over time in a context largely shaped by the needs of conventional students. Today, these procedures require modification if they are adequately to accommodate the part-time students who wish to take classes at night as well as during the day, on or off the campus, and in degree or nondegree formats. Appropriate modifications to procedures, it is argued, would make obvious a suitable working structure:

> ADMISSIONS. Criteria which more adequately reflect an applicant's ability to participate successfully in university level education.
> REGISTRATION. Procedures to facilitate the entry and participation of the nonconventional student and to minimize segregation by age.
> ORIENTATION. Programs designed to meet the special information needs of conventional students participating in university programs.
> TRANSFER POLICIES. The development of flexible transfer policies to meet the needs of nonconventional students.
> SCHEDULING. The design of a more flexible schedule, on and off the campus, for both degree and nondegree programs.
> ENROLLMENT OPTIONS. The reconsideration of a variety of options to meet the needs of those not wishing to proceed to a university degree.

SUPPORT SERVICES. The provision of support services for non-conventional students such as an information and assistance center, counselling services, financial aid.
CREDIT FOR PAST EXPERIENCE. The reconsideration of policies regarding waiver examinations, credit by examination and the evaluation and offer of credit for competence gained through previous life experience.
CERTIFICATION. The review, expansion or modification of certification alternatives for participants in degree and nondegree programs.

Useful though such modifications may be, they do not readily suggest a structure for university continuing education likely to be functional for each of the major segments of continuing education program: credit courses, general education programs (which are extraordinarily varied in subject and format) and continuing professional education directed to specific clienteles.

Views vary, moreover, about where within the university responsibility for these modifications should be placed. Stern (1975) holds that part-time undergraduates and graduate students properly belong in the faculties from which they will receive their degrees; their control should thus be in the hands of the internal departments. But programs of general education, drawing as they do from the whole of the institution and from contemporary culture, can only be mounted adequately and on any substantial scale by an independent continuing education arm which functions on behalf of the entire institution. The third program area, continuing professional education, presents complications. Currently the largest element of university continuing education effort, its future has particular relevance to the institution. Were the university to remain indifferent to the education of professionals after they receive their degrees, it may well lose the pre-degree activity—professional preparation—which has been its birthright (Stern 1975, 14). Not infrequently, the framework of provision of continuing professional education is unstable, a state of uneasy and disputatious equilibrium between professionals and faculties and the continuing education divisions. Its organization is complicated by the vested interests of groups off the campus which include professional associations, bureaus of government and regulatory or licensing boards. Continuing professional education remains a highly political field of manoeuvre among protagonists on and off the campus. Where responsibility for it settles is likely to be determined by those who understand its political roots, who have devised policies which are perceived by those affected as likely to be of mutual benefit, and who are adroit at combination and compromise.

Closely connected and a key issue for the future is that of the centralization or decentralization of the continuing education function on the campus. There are three options from which to choose: the centralized, or the decentralized or the mixed/indecisive model. In the decentralized model, for historical reasons perhaps coupled to faculty aggressiveness, responsibility for elements of the university continuing education program are centered at different points on the campus. An extreme example is the pattern adopted by the University of Michigan: there, of seventeen schools and colleges, twelve maintain units engaged in continuing education within each of which function a total of twenty different, and for the most part autonomous, continuing education units. This pattern is described on the one hand as one congruent with the basic value systems of that University. Yet there may be less worthy motivations behind it: the assumption by faculties and departments of a continuing education role as a justification for the continuance of departmental staff resources or as a device to generate funds to serve their internal needs. Alternatively, it has been characterized as "organized chaos; anarchy; diversity without design; institutional mindlessness; adrift in a sea of overlap, duplication and competition" (Berlin 1976).

Historically, institutional drift has been towards decentralization, which has never been more evident than today, when individual institutions within university systems, and branch universities, faculties, departments and individual staff members all clamor for greater independence. But while decentralization is the academic impulse, centralization and coordination is the administrative impulse. It is the third model, the mixed, indecisive model, which has dominated university continuing education in North America. In it, and assuming a vacuum in institutional policy, it is the relative political strength of individual administrators which dictates events. In the absence of a conscious determination and implementation of policy, questions of economy or efficiency or educational consequences may be ignored. What today may motivate universities to consider the centralized model is the conclusion that this university responsibility, hitherto regarded as marginal, has now become too important to be relegated to the periphery of the institution.

A framework which assists the assessment of the issue of centralization and decentralization is provided in Knox's analysis (1977) which contrasts characteristic features of each of these two modes of organization as they affect these five groups: faculties within the institution; the continuing education division; the university's administrative apparatus; individual faculty members; and the individual and organizational clients of the institution for continuing education. A decision as to which of the two organizational forms, centralization and decentralization, is best suited to the university is obviously affected by the core administrative tasks inherent in the continuing education function: identification, planning and conducting of programs; operating the channels of communication between clients, staff and administration, the development and implementation of policies; the deployment of resources; and the character of the leadership role which each of the two organizational forms requires. The consequences of choosing either the centralized or the decentralized form are depicted in terms of outcomes as these: the degree of institutional commitment to the function; who wields influence over the budget assigned to the function; how the continuing education product is marketed; the impact of each of the two forms on administrative style; the effect of each on the autonomy of individual faculty members; the ease of access to the university of clients. Which of the two forms will produce the superior educational product will depend on what product or what outcome is wanted, on whether the institution is large, complex and specialized or small, compact and narrowly oriented to a particular clientele. A key criterion is whether it is centralization or decentralization which is likely to produce the optimum intellectual vitality in program and, at the same time, satisfy the administrative requirements of the institution.

Each mode has its advantages and disadvantages. Centralizing the function offers the likelihood of efficiency and cost-effectiveness: it may make possible standardization in administration and present the prospect of better operational control. It permits specialization within the range of continuing education activities, it may encourage flexibility, and it permits the achievement of balance among the university's continuing education offerings. It is likely to encourage a prompt response by the university to community needs and may facilitate the provision of more effective support services to continuing education. It avoids the likelihood of duplication and confusion in relationships or contacts between the university and an external client group. Much of the university's continuing education program is interdisciplinary and it may be that centralization of the function may encourage interdisciplinary cooperation. Finally, through centralization of the function, the advocate voice of the part-time student may be more clearly heard. The principal disadvantage of centralization of the function is the consequent separation of the staff of the continuing education unit from the rest of the institution — the creation of a kind of second-class academic citizenship. In a variety of ways both obvious and subtle — and to its disadvantage — the function is set at a distance from subject specialists within the faculties. Centralization may place too great dependence on too few individuals. Certainly it will be argued whether, in principle, the rigidly centralized provision of continuing education within the institution is consonant with optimal intellectual and creative vigor.

Among the advantages of the decentralized mode is the possibility it offers to continuing education truly to become an integral part of the institution. Responsibility for it would rest with internal departments which provided it and which, one might suppose, are those best able to assess its merit. Decentralization, it is proposed, might stimulate an initiative and an enthusiasm for university continuing education hitherto untapped on the campus. The placement of responsibility for continuing education at the departmental level could encourage flexibility, promptness in decisions and the most efficient use of faculty resources and executive time. Its most obvious disadvantage is the inevitable duplication of services, staff, effort and equipment required to maintain it; the facilities required by individual departments and faculties in order to undertake the function are unlikely to be uniform; and the effort required to discover and then to supervise staff who are both capable and willing to do this work. But the most serious defect of the decentralized mode lies in this homely truth: that what is everybody's responsibility is nobody's responsibility. A chief reason for what success university continuing education has enjoyed in the past has been the energy, enthusiasm and entrepreneunial skill exercised by those dedicated to it. That vigorous leadership might well be dampened in the decentralized structure.

Whatever the structure for the provision of university continuing education, one would expect that it would reflect the institution's unique history and traditions. But, in general, the criteria characterizing the optimal design would appear to be these:
- it will maximize the potential performance in continuing education of the whole university staff
- it will reduce the gap between the goals intended by the institution and those intended by its staff
- it will maximize communication and cooperation among all of those involved in the function
- it will enrich the working lives of staff members and enhance their satisfaction in their work
- it will favor autonomy, responsibility and accountability over regulation
- it will ensure continuity and stability in the performance of the function.

Kipling has it that "there are four-and-sixty ways of constructing tribal lays, and every single one of them is right" which is clearly true of the structuring of continuing education on the campus. But the balance of argument appears to favor a centralized, professional administration of the continuing education function, directed by an appointee at the vice-presidential level sensitive to the community within which the institution functions, who has ready entrée to the presidential office and to the councils of the institution.

External Relationships in University Continuing Education

University continuing education does not function in a vacuum but in a loose partnership.

A half-century ago, there were fewer institutions of postsecondary education, many of which were not engaged in continuing education. Existing in isolation from one another, they negotiated their support individually from government and proceeded in their tasks quite independently. In sharp contrast, today's network of postsecondary education comprises a broad array of universities, colleges, technical institutes, vocational centers and special institutions, most of them incorporating a continuing education thrust which are linked less closely to government departments or quasi-governmental bodies. As Faure and others have concluded, we live now in a "learning society," a theme newly dominant in the literature of education: it is not selected groups in the society which ought to be educated but the whole population which ought to be the object of education.

But if the target audience for education is to be the whole population, some more sophisticated and rational linkage of educating agencies must be created than exists at present. In a British view, "if our free society is to survive we must have a true *system* of education, that is, one in which each of the parts feeds and supports the others. . . . But if such a system is to be created it calls for genuine partnership among all the contributors to education. . . . We can no longer afford to have schools, colleges, equipment that are treated as the private property of the staffs . . . [or] deny the community full use of the educational plant it has paid for . . . [and which should] share . . . in the devising of educational objectives and educational forms that will be relevant to *their* intentions and aspirations" (Jones 1975, 12). This theme is evident also in a position paper of the Adult Education Association of the United States which, in its set of forty-two goal statements, emphasizes recognition of the growing inter-dependence of adult-education-providing agencies, acceptance of the concept of education as a process which continues throughout life, endorsement of the expansion of opportunities to adult educators to increase their professional competence—and the determination to achieve cooperation among continuing education agencies, public and private (Adult Education Association of the USA 1967). In short, what is necessary are mechanisms through which the continuing education provided by a variety of institutions can most efficiently and effectively be channelled to meet the identified needs of adult learners.

A study prepared for the California legislature proposes four areas of study central to the improvement of institutional performance in continuing education. All require interagency cooperation:
- the analysis of needs in postsecondary education
- the cataloging of information about all existing educational resources, including the nature and purposes of programs offered, fees, methods, the location of services, admission requirements, etc.
- the centralization of sources of information about all the instructional equipment and products available throughout the jurisdiction

- the provision of effective publicity about postsecondary education or lifelong learning programs (Peterson, Hefferlin & Lon with collaborators 1975, 143-149).

The external relationships of the university in continuing education is an area of study which the university with its unique resources could well undertake. Moreover, it seems likely that such an analysis would assist the integration of adult education efforts within the community.

An obvious way for the university to make connection directly with the expanding network of adult education providers and indirectly with the adult learner — and one which provides a channel for its leadership potential — is participation in local or regional continuing education councils. Typically, the purposes of such councils are to

- identify and interpret educational needs
- develop new educational approaches and programs
- publicize and promote programs of all agencies
- cooperate on jointly sponsored projects
- coordinate adult education activities
- act as a clearing-house of information about adult education activities
- identify and interpret trends
- promote legislation, public interest, and financial support
- represent the adult education movement before the public
- eliminate duplication of program
- ensure that groups of potential students who have a legitimate call on continuing education service are not overlooked (Knowles 1960, 183).

But, in fact, without sustained institutional support such continuing education councils have been only modestly successful. Three weaknesses are chronic to them: the lack of consistent financial support; the lack of consensus on the specific goals to be achieved, and their persistent failure to gain the support of the important community agencies, regrettably, universities among them. Indeed, they are fragile associations with an apparent inability to speak with one voice on issues affecting their field (Verner 1962).

It is clearly demonstrable in North America that the visibility of continuing education has been heightened through shrewd entrepreneurship and innovative programming. But if major expansion is to be achieved in that field, Griffith (1976) argues, it can be brought about on a large scale only through legislative action, the end product of lobbying. The future of continuing education, that is, will be secured by the translation of expressions of public need into public policy by legislators whose sympathy and understanding is cultivated. But, and this is the rub, before such a campaign can be mounted and the necessary bridges and political alliances built, continuing education must first mend the fragmentation within its own ranks. At the root of this fragmentation and the consequent lack of coherence in the field is the fact that adult educators have come into the field from such a variety of different and often unrelated backgrounds that, even if the will existed, they would have difficulty in understanding one another. No common ground of philosophy or goals in adult education, a *lingua franca*, links one adult educator to another. The inevitable consequence is a competitive spirit reflected in duplication of effort, instead of a cooperative approach founded on a common point of departure and common objectives. A solution to this problem lies in building a cadre of professionals in continuing education through training. In training lies the beginnings of a common language, the roots of a common bond and, through these, the possibilities of interorganization cooperation (Campbell 1977b).

Finance and Accountability

How the university institution ought to structure itself to meet its continuing education responsibilities is a question intimately connected to another: how it ought to be financed. Invariably, the financial arrangements made for continuing education are unlike those in other sections of the university.

The type and degree of financial provision made for continuing education will reflect institutional conclusions about such basic questions as these: since the benefits of continuing education accrue both to the individual and to the society, what proportion of its cost should be borne by each? Self-supporting and a taxpayer though he may be, ought the adult learner to pay a higher proportion of the cost of his education than does the conventional student? From what source should programs requiring development capital (which may be self-liquidating) be provided? Is it reasonable to expect citizens geographically remote from the institution to pay higher fees? Out of the total budget assigned to the institution by governments, how ought the size of the share for continuing education to be determined?

The almost invariable case with respect to the university's non-credit programs for the adult student and frequently the case with respect to credit programs is that their financing is placed on a net basis: if it is foreseen that a course will not pay its own way it is cancelled. No other division of the university is required to support itself in this fashion. It is not a strategy which is justifiable in terms of organizational or economic principle; rather, it is an accident of historical development. This policy has its consequence. Citizens may well conclude—and it is their attitudes which are mirrored in legislatures—that in the university's judgment, the preferred clientele, the proper clientele, is the eighteen-to-twenty-four-old age group and that, despite changes in the society which make continued learning an imperative, the adult learner-taxpayer is an interloper merely to be tolerated. A specific consequence of this style of funding is to press university continuing education divisions to become peddlers of the popular. Indeed, its critics regard this principle of self-support, the financial undergirding of much of university continuing education, as a vicious system which forces universities to make education decisions with income as the major criterion and to neglect the very people who often need the educational services the most. Since the emphasis is placed on making money, the provision of continuing education to small business, teachers, social workers and low-income groups is inhibited and the focus becomes engineers, professionals, large corporations and upper-income citizens. In short, it puts the university's continuing education program out of balance (McNeil 1977).

One kind of institutional shortsightedness about the funding of continuing education is striking. Conceding that education has become a lifelong process and acknowledging that the university is uniquely qualified to contribute to meeting the need for continuing education, the institution stipulates that any expansion of continuing education programs require resources over and above those now available to it. That this financial posture presses university continuing education program towards commercialization and, almost certainly, to lower standards than ought to be acceptable can scarcely be denied. Certainly, as long as university continuing education is obliged to operate within the framework of an enrollment economy, just so long will it be frustrated in its attempts to redefine its mission in a society the character of whose educational needs change rapidly.

If, as seems evident, present patterns of funding militate against fulfillment of the university's unique and proper continuing education function, what remedies are possible? There appear to be three basic solutions. First, noting that part-time students, credit and noncredit, are the dominant constituency, the funding formula devised by government and administered by the institution might be amended to support the aspirations of adult learners. Secondly, the university's scale of tuition fees might ensure that the hourly rate of fees charged to part-time students in either credit or noncredit programs is no greater than charged to the conventional full-time student. Third, citizen groups should insist that students in university continuing education programs should not be denied access to loans and scholarships from sources internal and external to the university available to conventional full-time students.

A variety of supplementary considerations invite attention. One is the retention by the continuing education division of program "profits"—the surplus of revenue over expenditure—to subsidize subsequent high-risk educational ventures. Institutional fund raising campaigns, focused on those who now comprise the majority of their clientele, could profitably give emphasis to the provision of continuing education. Business and industry, aware of the continuing education program's direct usefulness to them, might be invited to give direct support to this university function. If related tax legislation were supportive, as for example, a matching of dollars, the likelihood of support would be enhanced. Greater attention might be given to presidential approaches to foundations for project seed money and to inviting the partnership of government in continuing education projects relevant to legislative concerns. Where the numbers of conventional students decline, institutions might well consider the reassignment of staff to continuing education duties. Finally, government might be invited to provide supplementary funding parallel to but separate from budgetary provision to institutions for the exploration of continuing education projects uniquely important to a region. Such an experiment in British Columbia in 1974, appears to have been a considerable success. There the government of the province provided a carrot of $2,199,973 in special grants to the University of British Columbia in support of the Premier's statement to the legislature that "if the universities wish to go out to the community, and take their professional skills and professional helps in a new form of education at the community level, we will help them through financing . . . on behalf of those people who desperately need higher education out there in the community" (Barrett 1974).

Since the financial lean years following the heady period of university expansion in the 1960s, the theme of accountability, the requirement to justify the efficient and effective use of resources, is heard more frequently. Not only do universities not rate a preferred status in government budgets which they enjoyed a decade earlier, their current expenditure has come under ever more keen review by government and public alike. An evaluation of the efficacy of the university's continuing education thrust will have its base partly in the mandate given it by the institution and partly in the reasonable expectations by its various constituencies of the university.

Staffing

Data characterizing university continuing education staff are scant. But a 1977 survey of chief administrative officers of continuing education conducted in the United States by the National University Extension Association of seventy-three land-grant and state universities, however, provides at least a point of reference. Of the continuing education units surveyed, about two-thirds used the title "continuing education" or "continuing studies" while a quarter continued to use the older term, "extension." About half of their chief administrative officers were designated "dean," one-third were "directors" and one in ten "vice-presidents" or "chancellors." More than one-third of these officers reported to a vice-president for academic affairs and slightly more than a quarter to a president or a vice-chancellor. The annual budget of the institutions surveyed ranged from half a million to forty million, the modal figure being one to two million annually. The number of full-time staff in each of these continuing education units stretched from nine to over three hundred, with an average of ninety-one persons. The salaries of one-fifth of the principal officers ranged from $23,000 to $26,000, while 28 percent of them received a remuneration of $38,000 to $41,000. Fifty-six percent of them held faculty rank; 48 percent were eligible for tenure and 69 percent had access to sabbaticals or other types of leave (Durnall 1977).

For the rank and file of university continuing educators, there is no parallel data though the kind of tasks they are called on to perform are well reported in the literature by Selman (1973a), Blaney and Foth (1979), Scott (1978), and Jensen and others (1964). Success in accomplishing their tasks is judged to require certain skills and attributes, among them these:
- skill in the design of learning projects appropriate to a variety of individuals and groups
- sensitivity to group processes and an understanding of leadership styles and roles
- a capacity for the discriminating observation of the community and sensitivity to its needs
- the ability to implement effective teaching/learning techniques and to evaluate the quality of the continuing education product
- an understanding of continuing education as a field of study and practice (Explorations in Adult Learning . . . 1970).

In addition to all of these, the principal continuing education officer requires an expert understanding of his institution. He must be a consummate politician sensitive to interfaculty tensions, who understands the values, fears and aspirations of the faculty, and who appreciates not only the totality of university concerns but continuing education within that context (Blaney & Foth 1979).

Not untypically, he and his associates may be viewed not as colleagues, that is, those acting according to the policies and spirit of the scholar, but as entrepreneurs who use the university as a base for educational retailing. Indeed, the university administration itself may regard its continuing education division merely as a device to buy public goodwill. Where institutional support evidenced through a carefully articulated set of purposes and policies does not exist, university-based continuing educators live in a state of uneasiness, unsure of their status within the institution and of their role. Privately, they may question whether what they do is important or whether they function merely as hewers of intellectual wood and drawers of academic water. While noting that others of their campus associates have secure career lines and acceptance by a peer group, they perceive institutional support for their own efforts in continuing education to be lukewarm, their share of institutional budget determined not by the needs of the function but by what is left over when other demands have been met (Godbey 1975). In the eyes of his academic associates, the continuing educator is a weak member of the academic household, one not belonging in the front room, who does not look or think or act like a scholar and who, because he does not fit, is properly relegated to middle-level management. In the judgment of the president of Simon Fraser University, "the absence of a strong professional identity for adult educators has contributed to their lack of acceptance . . . as has the paucity of high quality research in that area of study. Finally, the failure . . . on the part of continuing educators to develop and apply a sound conceptual basis for the practice of their craft undoubtedly has constituted another serious impediment to their establishment of a vigorous academic reputation" (Pedersen & Fleming 1979, 7).

The obvious remedy lies in the determination of the continuing educator himself to extend his competence beyond the conventional bag of organizational tricks into the theory base of adult education. Currently among university continuing educators, the "entrepreneurial-administrative-marketing" work model prevails. What is required is a deliberate shift to a "professional-academic model," one consistent with the university's emerging responsibilities in continuing education. No university adult education program will succeed as it ought without the involvement in it of staff who are intellectually and professionally the equal of their colleagues in the academic community. What is equally important is access by continuing educators to a satisfying career opportunity focused on the achievement of university goals (Council for Cultural Cooperation 1966; Campbell 1977b, Elsdon 1975; Knox 1979).

If continuing education is to become a vital component within the institution, administrative support at the topmost level is imperative. In those institutions in which continuing education has been enabled to play a significant role, there has been a president who was the prime mover, an articulate and persuasive spokesman in the senior deliberative councils of the institution. Within the continuing education division itself, it is the dean or director who sets the tone, who determines its quality and character. His leadership must be effective in several roles. Basic to it is the monitoring of programs, the proposal of innovations or the assisting of innovation proposed by others, the continuous improvement of instruction and the stimulation to needed research. Good communication—that building and maintaining of links with every segment of the university and with the principal elements of the community which the university serves—is vital because without it the continuing education function is isolated both from the institution and from its potential clientele. Because continuing education involves an intricate network of relationships, diplomacy is an essential element reflected in the continuing task of negotiating collaborative agreements and maintaining external relationships with a variety of offices. Finally, there is the role of advocacy, the ongoing interpretation of university role in continuing education. It is a task which demands vision, a capacity for the creative, the diplomatic touch—and, inescapably, moral courage.

But perhaps most important, what is required of the leader in continuing education, as of any leader within the university, is the will to broaden his intellectual horizons and progressively to develop his philosophy of education: in short, a commitment to his own continuing education. For as Norman Cousins (1974) remarks, it is the job of leaders to brood creatively about purpose and present future goals. Amidst the constant pressures of contemporary change, it is paralyzing to leadership to be unremittingly obliged to seek resources for the function for which he is responsible or to be required to give priority to routine administration rather than to ideas. In that circumstance, the prime casualty is thought.

Marketing Continuing Education

Continuing education has no captive clientele. Its constituency is the entire community. Those whom it serves are "volunteers for learning," the term coined in the massive study of adult education by Johnstone and Rivera (1965). Necessarily, then, the university continuing education division must catch the attention of its potential adult audience by marketing its product successfully. With the emergence in the last two decades of a broad assortment of alternative providers of continuing education, colleges, technical institutes, commercial organizations and public school boards among them, that market has become increasingly competitive.

Traditionally in institutions of higher learning, the concept of marketing, of spending money in advertising and promotion, has been anathema. Until recently, marketing strategies in continuing education have not gone much beyond the production and distribution of brochures and newspaper advertising. There has been little study of rationally structured approaches to it; yet merely to design courses without engaging public interest in them is to risk their eclipse in a welter of competitive items offered by a multiplicity of agencies. Sound tactics in the marketing of university continuing education are based on certain assumptions about its future development. If, as is estimated, adult learning requirements will be largely for noncredit university continuing education, the demand factor will largely comprise the aggregate of individual consumer preferences for particular courses rather than for sequences of courses, as is characteristic in a degree program. Further, consumers of continuing education—as in recent years, consumers of all products—will examine ever more critically what they are offered and seek courses demonstrating high quality in content and expertise in process. Good quality will become an essential.

Different groupings of continuing education courses call for different marketing strategies. But whatever the strategy chosen, the ends to be achieved are these:

- the provision of a range programs to a variety of segments of the community
- experimentation in subject areas which, in ordinary circumstances, would not be considered
- the penetration of markets which otherwise might be considered too remote

To be done well and in a manner appropriate to the institution, effective marketing requires the investment of money, the guidance of those expert in its techniques and acknowledgement of two caveats: that the negative image of contemporary hucksterism be avoided; and that marketing not itself influence institutional objectives.

Determining the course fee is an essential part of the marketing strategy. In university continuing education, there is rarely an established relationship between extramural and intramural tuition fees. Typically, tuition fees for each continuing education course reflect a synthesis of budget data including costs and projected revenue. In some instances, the institution may charge the lowest fee consistent with a balanced budget; in others, the fee is set at the maximum which it is judged the consumer would be willing to pay. The consumer's decision to purchase a university continuing education course, it would appear, is not dependent solely on price (Lamoureux 1976; DeWald 1974). The length of the course is also a determinant as is the image of the institution offering it. Nor in the eyes of the consumer is "cheaper" necessarily "better"; indeed, the opposite may be true and the potential participant may well estimate the quality or value of the course to him in terms of its price.

Other tactics in the pricing of continuing education courses include the determination of "price thresholds": the upper and lower price bounds perceived by the consumer to be "acceptable" or "fair." The consumer, perceiving inflation at work elsewhere in the economy, is willing to accept upward changes in the price of continuing education courses particularly if his income has tended to rise at a faster rate than course fees thus leaving him a greater discretionary income. Since an increasingly large number of participants — particularly those drawn from the business, technical and professional area — have their fees paid by an employer, the institution can be more aggressive in its pricing policies in these areas. Much of a university's continuing education program presents goods to the consumer which are difficult to compare with alternative purchases in terms either of character or price. But as with other goods, the consumer having found what he considers to be the "right" course is not unduly concerned about the price.

The application of another marketing technique, market segmentation, has the potential to enable postsecondary institutions to identify and subsequently to exploit hitherto unserved segments of the market. Market segmentation involves the subdivision of the market into homogeneous subsets of potential consumers to whom programs may be specifically addressed. Such an approach, to a specific, potential adult clientele, is illustrated in a booklet, *A University Degree - A Second Chance at 21 Plus* (1977), jointly issued by the Universities of Manchester, Liverpool, Leeds, Sheffield and Birmingham. Sympathetic in tone and helpful in the information it provides, it makes clear to the intending adult student that his maturity and experience will be recognized, that his past educational attainments will be evaluated realistically, that he will receive adequate counselling, and that he will have access to grant assistance. It is precisely the lack of such assurances to potential adult learners which has inhibited their pursuit of education in the past.

Research

"One of my fundamental assumptions," says Chris Argyris (1974, 62), "is that the most important resource an organization has is valid information."

If a substantial stock of valid information is a prime resource, then, at least in the past, continuing education has been impoverished indeed. The weakest features in the structure of university continuing education are the absence of reliable data, inattention to research and indifference to the development of continuing education as a professional field. Mezirow's judgment (1971, 135) is accurate: "There are few more pervasively debilitating influences in the professional field of adult education . . . than the absence of a body of practically useful theory upon which priorities in research, program development, evaluation, and professional training may be predicated."

Because continuing education in the community is no small enterprise and is, indeed, one which consumes many millions of dollars in service to hundreds of thousands of learners, it might be assumed that the university now supports this phenomenon with serious study. Yet as Stager and Thomas (1972) report, relatively little critical attention to goals, program design, methodology and evaluation is evident and the character of research is rudimentary: "The descriptive method is highly prevalent . . . [there is] almost a total lack of experimental and theoretical research. The survey method . . . is one that appears to be used most frequently . . . the way of summarizing and treating data and is almost entirely limited to frequencies and percentages of responses. Few studies indicate that a thorough review of relevant literature has been conducted." There is only a meager listing of continuing education materials in the Harris (1965) compendium, "A Bibliography of Higher Education in Canada"; equally unfortunate is this fact: that Canada is the only major modern country in the world which does not have a journal of national distribution recording the nation's adult education research.

In the U.K., a 1973 enquiry into continuing education, the Russell Report, concluded that significant research in the U.K. of a kind which generates pertinent theory and tests its application was modest indeed in its volume. But in the United States, particularly within the last decade, serious attention has been given to research in this field by universities and foundations and, significantly, to mechanisms for its dissemination, chief among them ERIC (Educational Resources Information Center). But the application of that research is not generally characteristic in university continuing education divisions, where practice is more likely to arise out of tradition or to reflect random influences. Pressured by their marginal status in the institution, the focus of continuing education practitioners is the advancement of their field through political and economic tactics rather than through systematic enquiry.

Knowles (1973, 302) views research needs in such a developing field of social practice as continuing education as progressive:

SUCCESSIVE PHASES OF DEVELOPMENT	RELEVANT RESEARCH
Definition of the Field	Survey-descriptive studies Census studies Case reports Demographic studies
Differentiation of the Field	Comparative studies Exploratory studies Reports of artistic experience Need analysis
Standard-Setting	Normative-descriptive studies Evaluative research Instrumental studies
Technological refinement	Experimental research Case studies Theory-building Action-research

Successive Phases of Development (cont'd)	Relevant Research (cont'd)
Respectability and Justification	Historical studies Biographical research Field-evaluative studies Survey-descriptive studies Comparative studies
Understanding of the Dynamics of the Field	Institutional studies Environmental studies Force-field analysis Systems analysis Prediction studies

Much of the existing body of research lies in the first three of these phases.

Characterizing what is appropriate in research in this field are such criteria as these:
- It deals exclusively with adults.
- It is directly related to adult education.
- It investigates real problems of concern to the field and/or the discipline.
- It contributes to an explanation of the phenomena with which adult education deals.
- It tests the applicability to adult education of knowledge derived from other disciplines.
- It is directly related to previous research and contributes to the systematic accumulation of knowledge about educating adults.
- It contributes to the professional education of leadership in the field at the graduate level (Verner 1978, 47).

Advice as to what the priorities in research into continuing education ought to be is in no short supply. One taxonomy identifies three inter-related themes within which the most significant problems are held to lie: the adult as learner; the adult's response to social-cultural phenomena; and the adult education enterprise (Kreitlow 1968 and 1970). Figure 3 graphically represents the major functional areas of research and development central to the improvement of the field thus (*Higher Education Management* 1971):

FIGURE 3
Functional Areas of Research and Development
in Higher Education Management

```
            Goal
            Setting

Evaluation  Communication  Program
            Base           Planning and
                           Resource
                           Allocation

            Execution
```

Within the framework of these taxonomies, specific contemporary research requirements are identified in several reports (College Entrance Examination Board 1978; Society for Research into Higher Education 1978; National Advisory Council on Extension and Continuing Education 1977; Peterson, Hefferlin & Lon with collaborators 1975; Selman 1973b).

Hand in hand with research goes the development of the professional field of continuing education, "professional" used in the sense of demonstrable technical competence flowing out of a theory base. Currently, the orientation of leadership in continuing education tends towards the immediate and the practical guided by administrative expediency rather than to a long-term development of the field through the creation of a body of underlying theory. That posture contributes to the failure of the field to present a coherent claim for public attention and support (Campbell 1977b). But what has been earlier noted bears repeating: if a clientele of adult learners whose level of education is substantially beyond what it was two decades ago is to be expertly served, if productive coordination even among the major institutional providers of adult education is to be achieved, if duplication in continuing education activities is to be avoided, if the omission of important learning opportunities for adults is to be rectified, if continuing education is to gain a necessary cohesiveness, training must supplement the native skills which continuing educators bring to their field. On those engaged in continuing education as professionals, the demands made are those of other professionals: keeping abreast of the literature; accepting the discipline of research; and sharing common interests with colleagues through professional associations.

It is the university, through perspicacious individuals within it, which has first identified and then adopted promising areas of study and reified them as distinctive programs of study. The university institution has a unique responsibility. It is the university to which continuing educators reasonably look for leadership in the development of their field through the provision of research.

The Responsibility of Government

Although the creation within the university itself of systematic and rational mechanisms for the provision of continuing education offers promise, substantial advance is unlikely to happen unless the support of government is coupled to the initiative of the university. It is all very well to state, as official reports frequently do, that "the expansion of opportunities for further education — usually referred to as adult or continuing education — and the acceptance of public responsibility for their provision are as urgent as was the establishment of the provision for elementary education almost a century ago" (Alberta 1972, 59). But a Council of Europe report (Council for Cultural Cooperation 1966) warns that recommendations about the development of continuing education are unlikely to command attention except where they are clearly recognized by government as urgent and contributive to social well-being. Indeed, most major contemporary North American examinations of continuing education are quite specific about the vital role of government in continuing education development. Willard Wirtz, in his former role as U.S. Secretary of Labor, for example, concerned with what he perceived as an unsatisfactory relationship between education and work and recognizing that what needs to be changed cannot be changed without the partnership of government, emerging requirement for professionalism in continuing education; that is, for that technical competence which proceeds out of a sound theory base. University leadership in research will lend coherence to the field and enable a more effective service to its clientele of adult learners.

The design of university continuing education and the provision of mechanisms for the delivery is the responsibility of the university. Yet without the support of governments of the concept of continuing education, the university's potential is unlikely to be completely realized.

6 University Continuing Education
The Prospect

The model for today's university was created in another age, with some of its ancient ceremonials surviving to the present. Now, as then, its goals are the preservation and dissemination of knowledge. But in the clientele it serves and the styles of its service, the university is not immutable. Indeed, the contemporary university is vulnerable in the face of discontent of government at its cost, of students with its relevance, and of employers with its product.

A popular conviction is that the university undertakes change scarcely ever and with the greatest reluctance. Yet over a half century, Canadian universities have made significant adaptations to pressures. The presidential role in governance was diminished suddenly in favor of the staff. Today's university consults with the student body to a degree which earlier would have been unthinkable. At the unexpected request of government, universities changed their procedures quickly and drastically in order to accommodate veteran students after World War II and dramatically magnified the attention paid to research. As well, universities have created new agencies to meet particular needs at particular times, for example, divisions of rehabilitation medicine instituted to serve those caring for the needs of polio and thalidomide victims. University libraries have readily incorporated in their processes such new technology as the micro-fiche and the silicon chip to such a degree, indeed, that wags sometimes term its work a "fiche and chip" service. Slowly, change has taken place; the issue is less institutional unwillingness to change but rather the extraordinary acceleration in the rate at which adaptation by universities is required.

Technology and social change has made plain to all postsecondary institutions this sober truth: that education must realistically be conceived as a process which continues throughout life. The universities' thrust in continuing education, developed as it has been in the crucible of experiment in the market place, has already been of immense practical service. But changes are necessary to it. Winston Churchill once remarked of a contemporary that, although his purpose was to save the world, his method was to blow it up. Fortunately, university continuing education is well-established and offers a solid base on which to rebuild. In this chapter, the intention is to estimate public expectations of higher education and in light of those expectations, to propose strategies for change in the university's conduct of the continuing education enterprise. The key issues in contemporary university continuing education will be recapitulated since it is these which provide a point of departure for the formulation of institutional policies.

Public Expectations of the Universities

If there is not in the making a revolution in higher education, there is abundant evidence which presages sharp shifts in its directions.

"The most vivid truth of the new age," wrote Margaret Mead, is "that no one will live all his life in the world into which he was born, and no one will die in the world in which he worked in his maturity." What is plainly evident to those who work in science or technology or the arts is that change occurs at ever shorter intervals. Today's centenarian has seen in his own span sweeping technological advances greater than took place in all of the accumulated past, his life shaped by the age of electricity, the automobile age, the aviation age, the electronic age, the atomic age, the space age and the computer age.

Technological advances have created an environment characterized by social changes most of which have inescapable relevance to university role. There is anxiety about the physical environment, the state of the economy, the distortion of inflation and the security of employment. Public distrust grows especially, distrust of "experts," of large organizations, of government and its bureaucracies. Disenchantment with public services is evident especially in education, welfare and health, not only because of their cost, but because of their seeming incapacity to adjust to new realities. Unease is widespread that the long-forecast age of leisure has indeed arrived, but in the guise of "structural unemployment." The very course of adult life is changing. Its phases of schooling, marriage and career have become blurred; separation from one's employment and mid-career change have become distinct and frightening possibilities; early retirement or semi-retirement or the requirement of a distinctly different lifestyle today replace the relatively rigid but perhaps more placid life patterns of a quarter-century earlier. Mixed into this amalgam of social patterns are demographic changes: a strikingly different urban-rural balance; shifts in the distribution of population among regions; and an inexorable expansion in the proportion of older people.

Unmistakably, as the nation has grown affluent, access to its resources—among them its educational institutions—has come to be regarded as a matter of right. A consequence of shifts in population ages, the size of the conventional student body on the campus is declining; its members seek more flexible, more diverse modes of learning; and present patterns of employment—which may well be permanent—press the student to combine learning and working. Educational orthodoxy is thus confronted with new demands, and their obverse, new opportunities. Other more profound changes are projected. Eric Ashby, sometime Master of Clare College, Cambridge, concedes that "forces from outside the university, which formerly only had a marginal effect upon the evolution of the university, are now likely to exert a powerful influence on this evolution. Governments which hitherto have been content to leave universities alone are now tempted to exert more and more control. Clearly, protestations about this are useless. Universities are now very expensive to run. None of them can hope to survive without patrons . . . the patron is now the man in the streets; universities must negotiate with him and establish new conventions to safeguard what they have inherited" (Ashby 1974, 7–8). Universities, he continues, are costly; their bills have to be paid and it is only proper that the campus should be shared with a larger public which—making no pretense to be intellectuals—should in the national interest have some understanding of the rigors of intellectual discipline as practiced by scholars. But with this proviso: that the university give unashamed, preferential treatment to the genuine scholar, one willing to submit himself to a stern regimen (Ashby 1967).

There is reason to speculate that if the contemporary university is to have a future, the process of its adaptation must be speeded up which is the view of Ashby's equally distinguished Oxford colleague, A.H. Halsey (1973): "if the university is devoted primarily to the nurture of the intellect it may be that it is thereby fated to occupy a very small place in the system of higher educaton . . . it can be socially defensible only if its intellectual product is not seen to bolster economic inequality and social hierarchy." Adding his own emphasis to the theme, the distinguished American educator, John W. Gardner (1968a, 106) observes that "our institutional arrangements for life-long education are ridiculously inadequate. Most educational institutions are still designed for young people who have nothing else to do. They are ill-suited to men and women who must fit their learning into a busy life." That judgment is expanded by a leading Canadian scientist and educator, Kenneth Hare (1969, 1–4): "I believe . . . that universities in the future will gradually become places of lifetime resort . . . that [education] will, in future, be a life-long thing, as this country's universities become what they ought to be; not simply places of accommodation for the young; not training schools for the high-school leaver; not the sheltered retreat of scholars; but the real core of an advanced society, where ideas, skills, argument, moral judgments and innovations can jostle together with the people in society who use them." That these inter-related themes are dominant internationally is apparent in a 1978 UNESCO report and in the proceedings of the 1978 Commonwealth Universities Congress. "The question no longer [is] whether the university should concern itself with being relevant to society's needs, but how it could do more to serve its national—and global—community without diminishing its traditional role" (Cocking 1978, 15).

In some part at least, these views crystallize the aspirations of the public for their universities. Yet, despite their tone of urgency, apathy or resistance to adaptation in academe is not untypical and is based, it would seem, on four fears: that the intellectual component of the university will become diminished; that university expertise will be compromised by value commitments; the possible threat of metamorphosis of the university from an institution characterized by objectivity to one dominated by subjectivity; and the impact of all of these on its autonomy (Brubacher 1970). Thus two competing views compete. One is that public service, including university continuing education, is an inappropriate and irrelevant function of the university which is inconsistent with basic academic responsibilities. The other is that, of all institutions, the university has the greatest responsibility to be a shaper of society and that it ought to prepare itself to reach out into the larger community through continuing education. Meanwhile, these opposing views unresolved, there is some evidence to suggest that the public perceives the university to be out of touch with society's needs. The president of a major corporation speculates whether universities are even aiming at the right market. "Are we pitching our efforts to the most promising age group?" he asks. "Is the average full-time student of today sufficiently mature to pursue the excellence we should be asking of him or her? I doubt it." A chief officer of a major foundation observes of the university and its apparent goals that "as a fund-dispenser as well as a member of the public, I instinctively look for where I think the most creative energy in our society is to be found, and I cannot, in all honesty, say that I find it at present in our universities" (Thackray 1978, 11).

Such as institutional posture of conservatism in the face of desired change has its potential consequences which are detailed in an essay, the very title of which is instructive, "From Private Domain to Public Utility" (Corry 1970). The universities, Corry argues, live on collective resources assembled by government from the taxpayer and they must thus serve the collective needs of the community. Unless the valuation by the university of these collective needs and the priorities among them approximately coincides with that of government, then government will call the tune. Government, after all, survives by reflecting public opinion and its tune will conform to its estimate of public opinion. The real enemy of the universities is not government but indecision within academic ranks and reluctance to chart a new course.

An abundance of advice is available from a host of sources as to fresh directions the university might follow. Indeed, perhaps, the problem is not a lack of advice but rather a superfluity of it: as an OECD report (1976a) notes, university administrations have not been able to digest even a fraction of all the material that has poured in on them from commissions, councils, working groups, to say nothing of the other literature of educational policy. Because of their very profusion, recommendations to the university flow over it rather than into it.

About the university's capacity to adapt, experienced university leaders express doubts. Murray G. Ross (1978) concedes that the major issue confronting universities in the 1970s was not cash but confidence: a lack of confidence by the public that universities are useful and responsible and a lack of confidence by the faculty in the university as a viable and valuable social institution. Part of the problem is the difficulty in getting faculty to recognize and accept the need for change; but as the Association of Commonwealth Universities was recently advised by an industrialist, "institutional arthritis" is inimical to innovation. John B. Macdonald (1978) argues that universities have become democratized to the point of paralysis. Partly, this is a product of institutional ambivalence as to whose goals should prevail: whether those of the institution or those of the society (Horowitz 1979). Partly, it reflects the historical roots of a society which has been reluctant to plan systematically for the future, in which immediate tasks overshadow long-term concerns and which has been hesitant to undertake risk-oriented ventures, all reflecting a reluctance perhaps attributable to the Protestant ethic which made planning seem an act of arrogance if not actually Marxist! (von Zur-Muehlen 1979, 2). Partly it is because, organizationally, universities have come to resemble the bureaucratic maze described by Elliot Richardson (1976, 160): "the unwieldy creature had its own self-serving purposes, its own organic processes, its own insatiable appetites. Surrounded by a dense categorical jungle, protected by layers of bureaucratic barbed wire, and tended devotedly by interest-group representatives, it had become all but inaccessible to broadly based public opinion." But whatever the reasons, if universities have indeed become incapable of adaptation, their future role may be determined by politicians. Here, John W. Gardner's sober judgment (1968b, 4) warrants attention: "I believe that the colleges and universities should provide intellectual leadership with respect to [continuing] education, and that depends on their own creative activity in this field. If they ignore it, the movement will pass them by and leadership will go out of their hands. If that happens, I think they will have reason to regret it."

Strategies for Change

North American universities have coped well with expansion to meet increasing demand. But they have not been through the process of shrinking. Nor, aside from the brief influx of veterans following World War II, have they had to accommodate themselves to a different clientele. If adaptation to changed circumstances is to gain institutional acceptance, debate and decision are required which embrace the entire campus. Such debate might be most productive were it to begin with the goals of the institution itself and were it to center on an understanding of what it is that obliges fresh approaches to a new clientele. Without an atmosphere of receptivity culminating in acceptance and willingness to move in a new direction towards the service of adult learners, discussion will ultimately prove abortive (Gould 1972, 180). Houle (1972) observes that the awareness of a need for program reconstruction must reach a certain level of pervasiveness or intensity before it can spur a formal decision to act and that a sufficiently powerful momentum to drastic change is reached only when a widespread body of opinion concedes the need for reconstruction or when that view is held by some person in a position of key authority. That "key authority" may be the president of the university. But currently, that officer's capacity to lead is restricted by the structure of institutional government which diffuses power so broadly. Yet the president's office has the potential to influence change: it has easy access to centers of authority in the society; a ready audience in the community for presidential views; and access to discretionary funds. These form a potent arsenal undergirding his efforts to achieve a reconsideration of the university's mission, and which will recognize and support adult learners (Campbell 1977a).

Four strategies for achieving change are open to the president (Houle 1972). The boldest is simply to assume that a decision has been made and to move at once to identify and implement new objectives. A more gradual approach, based on the view that an assessment of the present is essential to sound decisions about the future, is to undertake a full-scale survey. Another strategy is to determine criteria of excellence and use them to measure performance in the function examined. A fourth strategy is to probe deeply into particular aspects of the function and to propose specific changes in those which seem most vulnerable.

The choice of strategy will be made in awareness that the university is a political institution, political in that it is through strategic and tactical maneuvering that power and control are obtained and consolidated. Necessarily, that choice will take into account these typical features of the political process:

> New policy choices are usually modifications and additions to existing policies. Where important departures occur, current programs and arrangements frequently serve as models.
> Policymaking on the campus is conditioned by the interests and intentions of government.
> The sources of policy options are diverse.
> The initial large number of policy options is winnowed to a smaller group of possible options. In that screening process:
> - proposals that are better supported by good data and lucid arguments fare better
> - the power and status of those who are the source of a policy idea are important considerations in estimating how well it fares
> - policy proposals which conflict with the political sub-culture will fare less well than those which are consonant
> - policy proposals which are useful to key political leaders in their efforts to maintain their positions are more likely to be successful
> - timing and fortuitous circumstances, may well affect the acceptance of a policy proposal (Gladieux & Wolanin 1976).

A possible strategy for reconstructing university continuing education is the formation of institutional consortia; for as Jacques Barzun (1968) suggests, "if the university is to save itself by making the changes it is already eager to make, it must act not singly but in groups." No university, it is implied, can by itself substantially modify its educational directions lest that act be seen as a dilution of its program and its credibility be thus depreciated. An opposing view is that an institution intent on expanding nontraditional higher eduction ought *not* to wait for the approval of others but should use its own authority to initiate programs, to cope with unusual student backgrounds, to come to terms with the use of unfamiliar learning resources, and to acknowledge and examine alien philosophical outlooks on learning (Keeton 1972).

Essential in a strategy for change in university continuing education is the cooperation of the publics which the university serves. Academics must undertake to listen to their stated needs and to recognize within them the implied needs both of government and of the people government serves. Not to recognize the feelings and aspirations of the people who support the institution is to play into the hands of its critics (Dalby 1976). Hesburgh and his colleagues in framing a strategy for the development of nontraditional education at the University of Michigan offer several practical proposals aimed at gaining public support for change. The development of community "offices," for example, contact points through which the institution could sample public opinion, and the attachment of "advisory committees" to individual programs of continuing education offered by the university can serve well. Not to be overlooked is the development by the university of the closest possible relationships with other postsecondary institutions and, as a university, doing whatever lies within its power to strengthen the educational capacities of its partners to serve adult learners (Hesburgh, Miller & Wharton 1973). Frequently, universities have not cultivated needed friendships until crises were at hand; but the political reality is that, if its influence is to be maximal, the university's fences should always be in good repair. In the United States, the great land grant universities have developed enormous influence within their states because they have proved themselves willing to provide the services the public needs. Mayhew (1970, 149) states the obvious and important: that universities reluctant to provide service to the public risk reducing their own ultimate potency. "Functioning political power," he observes, "is based on mutuality of service."

Whatever the strategy used for restructuring continuing education on the campus, a very considerable responsibility falls directly on university continuing education personnel. As a field of practice, continuing education, despite the criticisms of it recounted in these chapters, has achieved a level of success unimaginable three decades earlier. But educators of adults, satisfied with their accomplishments, ought not to assume that further advances can be achieved by continuing the trajectory of the kind of programs that have already been established (Houle 1977). Further progress seems likely to be through uncharted and difficult territory; it may mean reaching many people now isolated from the university and bringing the present plethora of offerings into coherent, rigorous but assimilable patterns of lifelong learning.

Formulating Continuing Education Policy

This is the thrust of this account: to remain vital, universities must systematically recognize emerging goals of society and adapt to meet them. All of society's agencies, universities among them, are subject to the iron law of utility: should they fail to provide the services which changed circumstances require of them, they will be superseded by agencies which are willing to do so. Social history is littered with examples of organizations which, unable or unwilling to grasp the meaning of the times, drifting, and accommodating to change too reluctantly or too late, have been left to wither.

Preceding the argument for adaptation for change, is this question: have universities the *capacity* to change and have they the *will* to change? The answer is unclear. True, there are some signs that Canadian universities are re-examining their responsibilities in continuing education. A 1981 report initiated by the President of the University of British Columbia acknowledges that, "Our society is undergoing major demographic, economic and political changes [which] will have an increasing impact . . . on universities" and indicates six major areas in which change—and what kinds of change—is needed to accommodate nontraditional constituencies. Another document, "Report of the Task Force on Mature Students" prepared by the Senate of the University of Alberta in 1983 acknowledges mature students as an important element of the university's clientele group and proposes sixteen ways in which they should be aided. Most current is a 1983 submission to a Royal Commission by the President of the University of Lethbridge

Royal Commission by the President of the University of Lethbridge which concludes that six necessary reforms are vital and lie within the capacity of universities:
- the commitment to interdisciplinary education
- the restoration of liberal studies to a place of central importance
- the refurbishment of faculties of continuing education and their placement at the center of university life
- the amendment of university structures in ways that might foster the cross-pollination of knowledge and intellectual congress across subject boundaries and beyond institutional precincts
- the "declaration of war" by the research community on unskilledness
- the revision of the traditional subject areas in such a way as to make "globality" a mature area of research analyses.

But such presidential proposals or senate recommendations are one thing; whether the community of scholars which is the university has the capacity or will to initiate substantial change is quite another.

Not infrequently, organizational policies are based on myth or tradition or surmise. In the university institution especially in times of change, policies ought reasonably to be the object of the continuing, cool-eyed scrutiny which academics, who control the institution, apply to agencies other than their own. Answers are needed. But questions precede answers. A reassessment of the university's role in the provision of continuing education to adult learners, the new majority on the campus, might profitably follow the five-phase pattern below. Considerations of these question, each flowing out of the chapters preceding, might jointly be tackled by university and government together with the community which pays the institution's bills:

THE CLIENTELE FOR UNIVERSITY CONTINUING EDUCATION

What geographic, economic, occupational, educational and other features characterize the clientele which the institution intends to serve?

What groups of learners within the university's potential constituency are currently unserved or underserved?

The education/training required by the university's clienteles of adult learners

What criteria ought to guide the selection of continuing education programs appropriate both to the institution and to its various constituencies of adult learners?

What research processes might most accurately identify the present and future learning needs of these constituencies?

How might coherence within the whole of the university's continuing education offerings be enhanced (with particular reference to the organization of instruction in sequenced units)?

What mechanisms for continuing consultation regarding programs between adult learners to be served and subject matter specialists within the university ought to be established?

The barriers impeding access of adult learners to the university

What new practices in the presentation of university continuing education programs (including publication of information about learning opportunities and enrollment options, scheduling, location, orientation sessions, counselling and referral services, daycare) might encourage adult learners?

What access to the university's library holdings is it reasonable to extend to adult learners in noncredit courses and to those engaged in independent studies?

Would "educational brokering" services be advantageous to both the university and to adult learners and, if so, how might they be initiated?

What criteria ought to govern the level and application of tuition fees?

What access ought the adult learner to have to university funds designated for bursaries and scholarships?

What recommendations might be made by the university to government regarding day-release, tax incentives and the financial support of adult learners?

In what ways is it possible to serve those geographically remote from the campus?

The design of the university's continuing education program

How might the articulation in clear, specific, operationally useful terms of the goals intended by the university in continuing education (which reflect its traditions, resources and the learning needs of the constituencies it intends to assist) serve the function?

What particular provision of continuing education, if any, ought to be made to the university's alumni?

What ought the relationship of the university to be to those professional groups, external to the campus, which present continuing education programs on the campus which they, themselves, now conceive and direct?

What review, if any, is necessary, of conventional admission requirements to degree and diploma programs, of practices in the transfer of credit, of the testing of previous educational achievement elsewhere, as they relate to adult learners?

What consideration ought to be given to securing seed money for experimental programs of continuing education from departments of government, business and professional groups, foundations, etc.

How might independent learners be supported by the university through the preparation and provision of learning materials (cassette tapes, video-tapes, slides, films, etc.)?

What potential does the university's summer school have in residential continuing education directed to adult learners and their families?

THE STRUCTURE WHICH WILL BEST ASSIST THE DESIGN, DELIVERY, AND SUBSEQUENT EVALUATION OF CONTINUING EDUCATION

How ought the factors following shape the structure of the continuing education function on the campus so as to optimize the university's capacity to achieve its goals: on-campus relationships; the needs of the clientele to be served; the teaching-learning methodologies to be employed; the collaboration intended with other post-secondary institutions; the degree of centralization or decentralization of the function; the requirement of access to senior university leadership and to university councils; the responsibility of faculty members in continuing education provision; marketing strategies to be employed; the periodic assessment of output in cost-benefit terms; the degree of responsibility for the approval of programs to be undertaken by the institution's academic councils; the intended role, status, and required professional preparation of continuing educators; the criteria intended to guide the selection, terms of service and remuneration of on-campus and off-campus instructors in continuing education programs; the provision of in-service training to instructors of continuing education programs?

Jointly with professional associations (and, perhaps, government), how might the university plan continuing education in the various professions and the institutional role it is to play?

What new delivery systems might most efficiently and effectively serve adult learners: consortia; off-campus learning centers; work-study combinations; applications of the mass media (radio, television, newspapers, telephone, computer)?

What criteria are to characterize excellence in university continuing education programs as a basis for their subsequent evaluation (and, in particular, those intended to meet the requirement of a license)?

What researches, in what order of priority, would best support university continuing education development?

What responsibility ought the institution accept for furthering continuing education as a field of study and practice through the provision of training?

What opportunities exist for the provision of university continuing education on a contract basis to corporations, professional bodies and community organizations?

What alternatives in the financing of university continuing education would most appropriately serve both adult learners and the institution?

This framework provides a practical basis for the review of the institution's continuing education function. As to the outcome of that review, perhaps couched in terms of policies, one concedes that because university institutions vary in their history, their community setting, and their resources, no single, standardized set of policies—"guidelines to action"—concerning continuing education can be expected to serve all institutions. Each will evolve those policies which best reflect its unique circumstances. The observable fact, further, is that wholesale change on the campus is rarely accomplished in a single, radical policy turnabout. To the contrary, substantial change is more likely to take place over time: a composite of small changes, one built on another, in a coral-like accretion.

The time is ripe to make a beginning.

For nearly a century, universities in Canada have engaged in the provision of continuing education to adult learners, some of it distinguished in its quality. Leadership in it has come sometimes from the top echelons of the university; but more often, continuing education has been shaped by those at a middle level convinced that the proper constituency of the university is not exclusively a narrow band of privileged youth.

In large part, the organization and delivery of continuing education is overshadowed by institutional preoccupation with this traditional clientele. But today, the numbers of adult students on the campus in part-time credit and formal noncredit courses exceed those of the conventional student body. Because of dramatic and irrevocable shifts in contemporary society, adult learners have become a permanent and substantial element of the university's clientele. Nontraditional students in higher education are different in their attitudes, their motivation, their experience and their requirements of education. Manifestly, the needs of this new majority in higher education, their proportions on the campus swelling, invite fresh consideration by the institution undertaking to serve them.

But if higher education is on the verge of such a reorientation, it is not one characterized by a commonly accepted ideology or plan of action. The advice of numerous enquiries into higher education, urging recognition of adult learners and modification in the provision of their education, has gone largely unheeded. Universities have tended to proceed, largely as before, on the basis of a rather rigid system based on the degree, and supported by formal entrance requirements, schedules, disciplines and credit. Indeed, perhaps, to the public, the university's attention may seem permanently focussed on structure rather than on purpose.

As do any of the institutions which society has created, the university must come to terms with emerging social needs or court irrelevance. Mutual support between the university and society is a condition of the survival of the university. Certainly, the university cannot neglect its age-old responsibilities in research and scholarship directed at an intellectual elite; but neither will it be permitted to ignore the aspirations of adults who equate lifelong learning with their development or, indeed, survival. The character of the university in the future will grow not out of the displacement of its historic functions. Rather, it will derive from new approaches to them, which in part reflect the new majority in its student body.

In the recognition of and service to an adult clientele, the university may well find solutions to some of the financial and organizational problems which presently threaten it. But the real barriers to change are not money or staff or facilities; rather the real barriers are subtle limitations in vision or in attitudes shaped by the traditions of the university as it was during the first half of this century.

The goals which the contemporary university holds for itself must today be consonant with the goals held by those external to the campus: professional bodies, government, business and labor and a host of other agencies for whom recurrent education is no longer a frill but an essential. The intent of this book is to encourage and facilitate the review by the university of its goals in continuing education and the formulation of policies better to serve its new majority of adult learners.

References Cited

Adult Education Association of the USA. 1967. "A Program for Action." Position paper. *Adult Leadership*, March.
Alberta. 1972. *A Choice of Futures*. Report of the Commission on Educational Planning in the Province of Alberta, W. H. Worth, Chairman. Edmonton: Queen's Printer.
American Association for Higher Education. 1979. *AAHE Bulletin* 3, no. 8.
Andragogues, 17th Summer School of. 1974. Papers presented. Porec, Yugoslavia. 1974.
Argyris, Chris. 1974. "Conversation with Chris Argyris." *Organizational Dynamics*, Summer.
Ashby, Eric. 1967. "The Case for Ivory Towers." In *Higher Education in Tomorrow's World*, edited by Algo D. Henderson. Ann Arbor: University of Michigan.
―――. 1974. *Adapting Universities to a Technological Society*. San Francisco: Jossey-Bass.
Association of Universities and Colleges of Canada. 1977. "The Role of the University with respect to enrollments and career opportunities, admission policies, continuing education and community colleges." AUCC Policy Studies No. 1 Ottawa. Mimeographed.
Athabasca University. 1979. "Athabasca University, A Distance Education, Open Learning University." Brief presented at the Alsands project hearings, Fort McMurray. Mimeographed.
Baker, Harold R. 1976. "Organizational Design Within University Extension Units: Some Concepts, Options and Guidelines." *Canadian Journal of University Continuing Education* 3, no. 1.

References Cited

Barber, Nancy. 1975. *Directory of Higher Education Innovation.* Boulder, Colorado: Western Interstate Commission for Higher Education.

Barrett, David. 1974. Budget speech to the provincial legislature, British Columbia, 11 February.

Barzun, Jacques. 1968. *The American University.* New York: Harper and Row.

Beck, Clive. 1977. "Teaching in Post-Secondary Education." *Social Sciences in Canada* 5, no. 4.

Berlin, Lawrence S. 1976. "Diversity Without Design: Continuing Education at the University of Michigan." *ACE Reporter*, Student Journal of the Graduate Program in Adult and Continuing Education, University of Michigan, Winter.

Billington, James A. 1968. "The Humanistic Heartbeat Has Failed." *Life* 64, no. 21.

Blaney, Jack and Foth, Dennis. 1979. "The Ideal Dean/Director?" *Canadian Journal of University Continuing Education* 5, no. 2.

Boyes, George H. 1959. "The Scope of Activities Proper to a University Extension Department." Proceedings of the Canadian Association of Directors of Extension and Summer Schools in Universities, University of Saskatchewan. Mimeographed.

Brubacher, John S. 1970. "The Theory of Higher Education." *Journal of Higher Education* 41, no. 2.

Brun, Paul. 1981. "76 Career-related Liberal Arts Skills." *Bulletin*, American Association for Higher Education, October.

Campbell, Duncan D. 1977a. *Those Tumultuous Years: The Goals of the President of the University of Alberta during the Decade of the 1960s.* Edmonton: University of Alberta.

———. 1977b. *Adult Education as a Field of Study and Practice: Strategies for Development.* Vancouver: Centre for Continuing Education, University of British Columbia and International Council for Adult Education.

———. 1979. "University Continuing Education: A Balance Sheet for the 1970s." Address to the Canadian Association for University Continuing Education, Toronto. Mimeographed.

Canadian Association for Adult Education. 1964. *A Canadian Policy for Continuing Education.* White paper on the education of adults in Canada. Toronto.

Canadian Association for University Continuing Education (formerly Canadian Association of Departments of Extension and Summer Schools in Universities). 1970. "Position Paper." June. Mimeographed.

Canadian Association of Departments of Extension and Summer Schools in Universities. *See* Canadian Association for University Continuing Education.

Carey, James T. 1961. *Forms and Forces in University Adult Education.* Chicago: Center for the Study of Liberal Education for Adults.

Carnegie Foundation for the Advancement of Teaching. 1967. *Sixty-Second Annual Report for the Year Ended June 30, 1967.* New York.

Carnegie Quarterly. 1977. "What Is the Next Thing I Want to Do With My Life?" Vol. 25, no. 2.

Carp, Abraham, Petersen, Richard and Roelfs, Pamela. 1974. "Adult Learning Interests and Experiences." In *Planning Non-traditional Programs*, K. Patricia Cross, John R. Valley and Associates. San Francisco: Jossey-Bass.

CAUT Bulletin. 1979. "New 'Core Curriculum' for Harvard." Vol. 26, no. 1.
Chase, Harold W. 1968. "Indifference, Smugness and Rigidity in Academia." In *Whose Goals for American Higher Education?* edited by Charles G. Dobbins and Calvin B.T. Lee. Washington, D.C.: American Council on Education.
Clark, Burton R. 1956. "Organizational Adaptation and Precarious Values: A Case Study." *American Sociological Review,* XXI, June.
Clark, Terry N. 1968. "Innovations in Higher Education." *Administrative Science Quarterly* 13, no. 1.
Clark, Warren. 1982. "Can Universities Meet Challenge of Increasing Participation?" *University Affairs,* February.
Clark, W., Devereaux, M.S. and Zsigmond, A. 1979. *The Class of 2001: The School-age Population—Trends and Implications—1961 to 2001.* Ottawa: Statistics Canada.
Cocking, Clive. 1978. "Universities Should Use Knowledge to Serve Mankind." *University Affairs,* November.
Cohen, Arthur M. 1969. *Dateline '79: Heretical Concepts for the Community College.* Beverly Hills, Calif.: Glencoe Press.
College Entrance Examination Board. 1978. *Lifelong Learning During Adulthood: An Agenda for Research.* New York.
_____. 1980. *Americans in Transition: Life Changes as Reasons for Adult Learning.* New York.
Commission on Colleges of the Southern Association of Colleges and Schools. 1973. *The Continuing Education Unit: Guidelines and other information.* Atlanta, Georgia.
Continuing Education Service. 1977. *Handbook of Criteria and Procedures for Continuing Education Unit Programs.* East Lansing, Mich.: Continuing Education Service, Michigan State.
Corbett, E.A. 1954. *Henry Marshall Tory, Beloved Canadian.* Toronto: Ryerson Press.
Corry, J. A. 1970. *Farewell the Ivory Tower.* Montreal: McGill-Queen's University Press.
Corson, John J. 1968. "Public Service and Higher Education: Compatibility or Conflict?" In *Whose Goals for American Higher Education?* edited by Charles G. Dobbins and Calvin B. T. Lee. Washington, D.C.: American Council on Education.
Council for Cultural Cooperation. 1966. *Workers in Adult Education: Their Status, Recruitment and Professional Training.* Education in Europe, section 3, Out of School Education, no. 5. Strasbourg: Council of Europe.
Cousins, Norman. 1974. "Thinking Through Leadership." *Saturday Review,* 16 November.
Cross, K. Patricia. 1978. *The Missing Link: Connecting Adult Learners to Learning Resources.* New York: College Entrance Examination Board.
_____. 1981. "Partnership With Business and the Professions," in *New Frontiers for Higher Education: Business & the Professions,* Current Issues in Higher Education no. 3. Washington, D.C.: American Association for Higher Education.
Dalby, Ronald. 1976. Speech as Chancellor of the University of Alberta to "The Friends of the University of Alberta." May. Unpublished.

Dalhousie University. 1976. "Report of the Committee on Part-Time Study and Extension." Halifax, N.S. Mimeographed.

Daniel, John S. and Umbriaco, Michael. 1975. "Distant Study in French Canada: The Tele-universite." *Teaching at a Distance*, no. 4.

DeMott, Benjamin. 1978. "The Thrills and Shills of Lifelong Learning." *Change* 10, no. 4.

Design for Democracy. 1956. Abridgement of *The 1919 Report* of the Adult Education Committee of the British Ministry of Reconstruction. London: Max Parrish and Co.

DeWald, Samuel C. 1974. *The Role of Marketing in Continuing Higher Education and Community Service.* University Park, Penn.: Pennsylvania State University. 1974.

Donnelly, Robert S. N.d. "Continuing Professional Education: An Appraisal." Report for the Division of Continuing Education, University of Massachusetts, Amherst. Mimeographed.

Drucker, Peter F. 1969. *The Age of Discontinuity.* New York: Harper and Row.

Dunkel, Harold and Fay, Maureen A. 1978. "Harper's Disappointment: University Extension." *Adult Education* 29, no. 1.

Durnall, Edward J. 1977. "The Status of Chief Administrative Officers of Continuing Education in Land Grant and State Universities, 1977." Durham, N.H.: Division of Continuing Education, University of New Hampshire, for the National University Extension Association. Mimeographed.

──────. 1978. "Noncredit Continuing Education: Guidelines for the future." *Lifelong Learning: The Adult Years* 1, no. 6.

Eddy, Margot Sanders. 1978. "Part-time Students." *ERIC/Higher Education Research Currents.* Washington, D.C.: American Association for Higher Education, June.

Elsdon, K. T. 1975. *Training for Adult Education.* Nottingham: University of Nottingham; and the National Institute of Adult Education.

"Explorations in Adult Learning and Training for Adult Education." 1970. Proceedings of a conference held in Cambridge, England. Mimeographed.

Faure, Edgar and others. 1972. *Learning to Be: The World of Education Today and Tomorrow.* Report of the International Commission for the Development of Education. Paris: UNESCO.

Financial Post. 1978. "Computers: Threat or promise?" 9 September.

Fordham, Paul. 1975. "The Political Context of Adult Education." Edited version of address to staff seminar, University of Southampton. Mimeographed.

Frandson, Phillip E. 1978a. "Man Does Not Live by Credit Alone." Address at The 5th Annual Conference on Open Learning and Nontraditional Study, Kansas City, Missouri. Mimeographed.

──────. 1978b. In *Continuum*, March 1977, as quoted in *Canadian Journal of University Continuing Education* 4, no. 4.

──────. 1978 approx. "Continuing Education for the Professions." Unpublished paper. University of California.

Gardner, John W. 1968a. *No Easy Victories*, edited by Helen Rowan. New York: Harper and Row.

──────. 1968b. "Agenda for the Colleges and Universities." In *Campus 1980*, edited by Alvin C. Eurich. New York: Dell Publishing.

Gaynor, Robert H. 1974. "Partners in Community Development: The City and the Urban University - A Community Perspective." *NUEA Spectator* 37, no. 17.

Gladieux, Lawrence E. and Wolanin, Thomas, R. 1976. *Congress and the Colleges: The National Politics of Higher Education.* Lexington, Mass.: Lexington Books.

Godbey, Gordon. 1975. "Staff Morale: A Brief Comment." *NUEA Spectator* 39, no. 20.

Gordon, Morton. 1974. "The Organization of Continuing Education in Colleges and Universities." *NUEA Spectator*, September.

Gould, Joseph E. 1961. *The Chautauqua Movement.* Albany: State University of New York Press.

Gould, Samuel B. 1972. "Less Talk, More Action." In *The Expanded Campus: Current Issues in Higher Education*, edited by Dyckman W. Vermilye. San Francisco: Jossey-Bass.

Griffith, William S. 1976. "Adult Educators and Politics." *Adult Education* 26, no. 4.

Groteleuschen, Arden D. 1979. "Evaluation." In *Adult Education Program Development and Administration*, edited by Alan B. Knox. San Francisco: Jossey-Bass.

Gunning, Harry E. 1975. "President's Report to Convocation." *Folio* 11, no. 49. University of Alberta staff bulletin.

Halsey, A. H. 1973. As quoted in "Are the Universities Facing Era of Decline?" *Times Higher Education Supplement*, 2 March.

Hare, Frederick Kenneth. 1969. Excerpt from "Address to 1968 Spring Convocation, University of Western Ontario." As quoted in *CADESS Newsletter* 1, no. 1.

Harrington, Fred Harvey. 1965. Quoted by J. M. English. "Some Economic Questions Concerning Lifelong Learning." In *The New Challenge in Lifelong Learning.* Resolutions and proceedings of a conference on the future role of the University in relation to public service. Los Angeles: Universitywide Academic Senate Committee on University Extension.

——————. 1977. *The Future of Adult Education.* San Francisco: Jossey-Bass.

Harris, Robin S. 1965. A Bibliography of Higher Education in Canada. Supplement 1965. Toronto: University of Toronto Press.

Harvey, Edward B. 1974. "Canadian Higher Education and the Seventies." *Interchange* 5, no. 2.

Hesburgh, Theodore M., Miller, Paul A. and Wharton, Clifton R., Jr. 1973. *Patterns for Lifelong Learning.* San Francisco: Jossey-Bass.

Hiemstra, Roger. 1977. "Future: Friend or Foe?" *Lifelong Learning: The Adult Years* 1, no. 2.

Higher Education Management. 1971. "Why a Center for Higher Education Management?" Vol. 1, no. 1.

Horowitz, Myer. 1979. As quoted in Folio, 15, no. 39. University of Alberta staff bulletin.

Houle, Cyril O. 1952. "Introduction." In *Universities in Adult Education.* Problems in Adult Education IV. Paris: UNESCO.

——————. 1972. *The Design of Education.* San Francisco: Jossey-Bass.

References Cited

———. 1977. In an address as quoted by Ronald Gross, "Toward a Learning Society." *Adult Education in Nova Scotia* 14, no. 1.

———. 1978 approx. "The Nature of Continuing Professional Education." Unpublished paper. University of Chicago.

James, Bernard J. 1971. "Can 'Needs' Define Educational Goals?" Unpublished paper. University of Wisconsin.

Jensen, Gale, Liveright, A. A. and Hallenbeck, Wilbur, eds. 1964. *Adult Education: Outlines of an Emerging Field of University Study*. Washington, D.C.: Adult Education Association of the USA.

Jessup, Frank. 1977. "Emerging Moral Issues in Society and Their Impact on Continuing Education in America." Address to the NUEA Annual Conference, Tucson, Arizona, 1977, as reported in *NUEA Newsletter* 10, no. 6.

Johnstone, John W. C. and Rivera, Ramon J. 1965. *Volunteers for Learning*. Chicago: Aldine Publishing.

Jones, H. A. 1971. "A Rationale for Adult Education." In *Teaching Techniques in Adult Education*, edited by Michael D. Stephens and Gordon W. Roderick. London: David and Charles.

———. 1975. "Partnership in a System." *Journal of International Congress of University Adult Education* 15, no. 1.

Kaplan, Anne C. and Veri, Clive R. 1974. *The Continuing Education Unit*. ERIC Report 94213. Washington, D.C.: Educational Resource Center.

Keeton, Morris. 1972. "Dilemmas in Accrediting Off-Campus Learning." In *The Expanded Campus: Current Issues in Higher Education*, edited by Dyckman W. Vermilye. San Francisco: Jossey-Bass.

Kegel, Paul L. 1977. "How Well Do We Serve the Adult Student?" *Lifelong Learning: The Adult Years* 1, no. 4.

Kerr, Clark and others. 1978. *Twelve Systems of Higher Education: Six Decisive Issues*. New York: International Council for Educational Development.

Knowles, Malcolm S., ed. 1960. *Handbook of Adult Education in the United States*. Chicago: Adult Education Association of the USA.

———. 1969. *Higher Adult Education in the United States*. Washington, D.C.: American Council on Education.

———. 1973. "Sequential Research Needs in Evolving Disciplines of Social Practice." *Adult Education* 23, no. 4.

Knox, Alan B. 1974. "Lifelong Self-Directed Education." In *Fostering the Growing Need to Learn*, edited by R. J. Blakely. Rockville, Maryland: Division of Regional Medical Programs, Bureau of Health Resources Development.

———. 1975. "Professional Competence: Means and Ends." *Professional Engineer*, November.

———. 1977. "Who Controls What?" Address at a conference on changing administrative models for continuing education, University of Chicago Center for Continuing Education.

———. ed. 1979. *Enhancing Professionalism in Adult Education*. SanFrancisco: Jossey-Bass.

Kreitlow, Burton W. 1968. *Educating the Adult Educator: Part 2. Taxonomy of Needed Research*. Madison: Wisconsin Research and Development Center for Cognitive Learning, University of Wisconsin.

_____. 1970. "Research and Theory." In *Handbook of Adult Education*, edited by Robert M. Smith, George F. Aker and J. R. Kidd. New York: Macmillan Company.

Kristjanson, A. M. and Baker, H. R. 1966. "University Extension." Report of the President's Committee on University Extension, University of Saskatchewan. Mimeographed.

Lamoureux, Marvin E. 1976. *Marketing Continuing Education: A Study of Price Strategies*. Occasional Papers in Continuing Education, no. 11. Vancouver: Centre for Continuing Education, University of British Columbia.

Lawson, Kenneth H. 1973. "The Justification of Objectives in Adult Education." In *Studies in Adult Education 5*. London: National Institute of Adult Education.

_____. 1975. *Philosophical Concepts and Values in Adult Education*. Nottingham Studies in the Theory and Practice of the Education of Adults. Nottingham: University of Nottingham; and the National Institute of Adult Education.

LeBreton, Preston P. and others, eds. 1979. *The Evaluation of Continuing Education for Professionals: A Systems View*. Seattle: University of Washington.

Lenz, Elinor. 1976. "The Humanities Go Public." *Change* 8, no. 1.

Linder, George. 1973. "The Trend Toward Compulsory Continuing Education in the Professions." *Dialogue* 1, no. 1.

Lumsden, D. Barry. 1977. "The Curriculum Development Process in Adult Education." *Adult Education* (UK) 49.

MacCormack, J. R. 1975. "Educating the Public: Universities and the Mass Media." *CAUT Bulletin* 23, no. 5.

McCourt, Edward. 1968. *Saskatchewan*. Toronto: Macmillan of Canada.

Macdonald, John. 1978. As quoted in "The Inside Track: Who's in Charge Here?" *Saturday Night*, October.

McGill University. 1966. "Interim Report of the Senate Committee on Extension." Montreal. Mimeographed.

McMaster University. 1970. "Report to Senate from Ad Hoc Appointments Committee re a Dean of Degree Studies in Extension." Hamilton. Mimeographed.

_____. 1977. "Outline of Consultant's Report to Adult Education Sub-Committee (Board/Senate Committee on Long Range Planning)." Hamilton, 1976, revised 1977. Mimeographed.

McNeil, Donald R. 1977. "Toward Greatness." Paper presented at The 10th Annual Leadership Seminar in Adult Education, Michigan State University. Mimeographed.

Macpherson, C. B. 1970. "The University as Multiple Fool." *CAUT Bulletin* 19, no. 1.

Manitoba. 1973. *Report of the Task Force on Post-Secondary Education in Manitoba*. Michael J. Oliver, chairman. Winnipeg: Queen's Printer.

Mansbridge, Albert. 1913. *University Tutorial Classes*. London: Longmans, Green.

Mayhew, Lewis B. 1970. "The Power of Higher Education." *Journal of Higher Education* 41, no. 2.

Meierhenry, W. C. 1977. "The Role of Media in Education." *Sightlines*, Spring.

Mezirow, Jack. 1971. "Toward a Theory of Practice." *Adult Education Journal* 21, no. 3.

References Cited

Moses, S. 1971. *The Learning Force: A More Comprehensive Framework for Educational Policy.* Publications in Continuing Education, Occasional Paper No. 25. Syracuse, N.Y.: Syracuse University.

Munroe, David. 1973. "Post-Secondary Education in Canada: A Survey of Recent Trends and Developments." In *Post-Secondary Education in a Technological Society,* edited by T. H. McLeod. Montreal: McGill-Queen's University Press.

Murchland, Bernard. 1976. "The Eclipse of the Liberal Arts." *Change* 8, no. 10.

Murray, Walter Charles. 1909. *The President's Report, 1908-09.* Saskatoon: University of Saskatchewan.

National Advisory Council on Extension and Continuing Education. 1975. *Equity of Access: Continuing Education and the Part-Time Student.* 9th Annual Report. Washington, D.C.

———. 1977. *Proceedings of the Invitational Conference on Continuing Education, Manpower Policy and Lifelong Learning.* Washington, D.C.

National Center for Education Statistics. 1976. *Participation in Adult Education, Final Report, 1972.* Washington, D.C: U.S. Department of Health, Education and Welfare.

———. 1978. *Participation in Adult Education, Final Report, 1975.* Washington, D.C.: U.S. Department of Health, Education and Welfare.

———. 1978b. *Noncredit Activities in Institutions of Higher Education for the Year ending June 30, 1976.* Washington, D.C.: U.S. Department of Health, Education and Welfare.

———. 1979-80. *Noncredit Activities in Institutions of Higher Education for the Year ending June 30, 1976.* Washington, D.C.: U.S. Department of Health, Education and Welfare, Preliminary Tabulations.

———. 1981. *Participation in Adult Education* (1981 tabulations).

National Center for Higher Education Management Systems. 1978. *Measures of Institutional Goal Achievement.* Quoted in *NUEA Newsletter* 11, no. 15.

National Task Force on the Continuing Education Unit. 1970. *The Continuing Education Unit.* Washington, D.C.: National Task Force on the Continuing Education Unit.

———. 1974. *The Continuing Education Unit: Criteria and Guidelines.* Washington, D.C.: National University Extension Association.

National University Extension Association. 1946. *University Extension Experiments in Community Self Help Education.* NUEA Studies in University Extension Education, no. 4. Bloomington, Indiana.

Nevison, Myrne. 1979. *Canadian Magazine.*

New York University. 1962. "The Mission of the Division of General Education and Extension Services." Submitted by Dean Paul A. McGhee. New York. Mimeographed.

Newfoundland and Labrador. 1968. *Report of the Royal Commission on Education and Youth for the Province of Newfoundland and Labrador* 2. St. John's, Nfld.: Department of Education.

Nova Scotia. 1974. *Report of the Royal Commission on Education, Public Services and Provincial-Municipal Relations.* Halifax, N.S.: Queen's Printer.

OECD. 1976a. *Reviews of National Policies for Education: Canada.* Paris.

———. 1976b. *Comprehensive Policies for Adult Education.* Paris.

_____. 1976c. "Education and Work in Modern Society." *Adult Training* 1, no. 3.

O'Keefe, Michael. 1977. *Adult Education and Public Policy.* Occasional Paper, Program in Education for a Changing Society. Cambridge, Mass.: Aspen Institute for Humanistic Studies.

Ontario. 1972. *The Learning Society.* Report of the Commission on Post-Secondary Education in Ontario. Toronto: Ministry of Government Services.

Open University. 1976. *Report of the Committee on Continuing Education,* Sir Peter Venables, chairman. Milton Keynes, U.K.: Open University.

Parkin, David H. 1975. "The New Hard Times: Radio and Television in Continuing Education." *CAUT Bulletin* 23, no. 5.

Pedersen, K. George and Fleming, Thomas. 1979. "Continuing Education Divisions and the Crisis of Success." *Canadian Journal of University Continuing Education* 5, no. 2.

Pelletier, the Hon. Gerard. 1968. When Secretary of State for Canada, in an address to the Association of Universities and Colleges of Canada.

Petersen, Renee and Petersen, William. 1960. *University Adult Education: A guide to Policy.* New York: Harper and Bros.

Peterson, Richard E. and Hefferlin, J. B. Lon with collaborators. 1975. *Postsecondary Alternatives to Meet the Educational Needs of California's Adults.* Final report of a feasibility study prepared for the California Legislature. Sacramento: Assembly Publications Office.

Pike, Robert M. 1970. *Who Doesn't Get to University—and Why,* Ottawa: Association of Universities and Colleges of Canada.

_____. 1978. "Part-Time Undergraduate Studies in Ontario." In *Innovation in Access to Higher Education,* Robert M. Pike, Naomi E. S. McIntosh and Urban Dahllof. New York: International Council for Educational Development.

Pilkington, Gwendoline. 1974. "A History of the National Conference of Canadian Universities, 1911–1961." Ph.D. dissertation. On microfiche, National Library of Canada, Ottawa.

Quebec. 1965. *Report of the Royal Commission of Inquiry on Education in the Province of Quebec,* part 2. Alphonse-Marie Parent, chairman. Quebec: Government of the Province of Quebec.

Richardson, Elliot. 1976. *The Creative Balance: Government, Politics, and the Individual in America's Third Century.* New York: Holt, Rinehart and Winston.

Rockhill, Kathleen (Penfield). 1976. "The Mystique of Certification, Education and Professionalism: In the Service of Whom?" In *Certification, Credentialing, Licensing and the Renewal Process.* Proceedings of a conference sponsored by the Northwest Adult Education Association, Washington Continuing Education Association and ERIC/Clearinghouse in Career Education, Seattle, Washington.

Ross, Murray G. 1978. As quoted in "The Issue is not Cash but Confidence." *University Affairs,* November.

Ruyle, Janet and Geiselman, Lucy Ann. 1974. "Non-Traditional Opportunities and Programs." In *Planning Non-Traditional Programs,* K. Patricia Cross, John R. Valley and Associates. San Francisco: Jossey-Bass.

Sapper, Laurie. 1975. "Adult Education in Britain: The Open University." *CAUT Bulletin* 23, no. 5.

Saturday Review. 1978. "Lawyer, teach thyself." 10 October.
Savicevic, Dusan and others. 1966. *Osnovi Andragogije.* Sarajevo: Zavod Za Izdavanje Udzbenika.
Scott, Robert A. 1978. *Lords, Squires and Yeomen: Collegiate Middle-Managers and Their Organizations.* AAHE-ERIC/Higher Education Research Report No. 7. Washington, D.C.: American Association for Higher Education.
Selman, Gordon R. 1973a. "What Future for University Continuing Education Units?" *Dialogue* 1, no. 2.
──────. 1973b. "A Member's Opinion: An Organization for the Study and Development of Adult Education." *Dialogue* 1, no. 2.
──────. 1978. "All Things Are Ready, If Our Minds Be So." Paper presented at a conference on contemporary issues in adult education, University of Alberta, Edmonton, March.
──────, and Sheats, Paul H. 1968. "Recommendations to the Faculty and Administration of the University of Lethbridge for a Program of Continuing Education." Lethbridge. Mimeographed.
Shaw, Nathan C., ed. 1969. *Administration of Continuing Education.* Washington, D.C.: National Association for Public School Adult Education.
Shulman, Carol Herrenstadt. 1975. *Premises and Programs for a Learning Society.* ERIC/Higher Education Research Report No. 8. Washington, D.C.: American Association for Higher Education.
Small, James. 1975. "Senate Report on the Future of the Extension Function: A Reaction." *New Trail* 5, no. 5. University of Alberta magazine.
Smith, R. C. 1973. "The Open University of the United Kingdom." In *Post-Secondary Education in a Technological Society,* edited by T. H. McLeod. Montreal: McGill-Queen's University Press.
Smith, Richard D. 1974. *Patterns of Innovation: An Inventory of Non-Traditional Instructional Activities* 2. Indiana: Purdue University.
Society for Research into Higher Education. 1978. "Higher Education into the 1990s: A Response." Paper resulting from a conference, London.
Stager, David A. A. and Thomas, Alan M. 1972. "Continuing Education in Canada." Preliminary draft. Unpublished. Toronto: Institute of Policy Analysis, University of Toronto.
Statistics Canada. 1974. *Population Projection for Canada and the Provinces, 1972–2001.* Catalogue 91–514. Ottawa: Statistics Canada.
──────. 1979. *From the Sixties to the Eighties: A Statistical Portrait of Canadian Higher Education.* Ottawa.
Stern, Milton R. 1975. "The Invisible University." *NUEA Spectator* 39, no. 22.
──────. 1976. "Compulsory Continuing Education for Professions, or the Gold Rush of '76." In *Certification, Credentialing, Licensing and the Renewal Process.* Proceedings of a conference sponsored by Northwest Adult Education Association, Washington Continuing Education Association and ERIC/Clearinghouse in Career Education, Seattle, Washington.
──────. 1977. "Academic Politics: Knowing What You Want and How to Get It." Paper delivered at conference on changing administrative models for continuing education, University of Chicago Center for Continuing Education.
──────. 1979. "At A Slight Angle to the University." Address to the NEH-NUEA Conference on Continuing Education in the Humanities, Memphis, Tennessee.

Symons, T. H. B. 1975. *To Know Ourselves*. Report of the Commission on Canadian Studies, vols. 1 and 2. Ottawa: Association of Universities and Colleges of Canada.

Tawney, R. H. 1966. *The Radical Tradition*. Harmondsworth, Middlesex: Penguin Books.

Thackray, James. 1978. As quoted in "Are Universities Fulfilling Needs of Business?" *Financial Post*, 13 May.

Trent University. 1974. "Report of the Senate Committee on University Planning." Peterborough, Ont. Mimeographed.

UNESCO. 1978. "UNESCO Committee of Experts Analyse Ways of Integration of Lifelong Education into University Life." *Higher Education in Europe*. Bucharest: CEPES, May-June.

———. N.d. *Recommendation on the Development of Adult Education*. Adopted by the General Conference at the 19th session, Nairobi, 1976. Ottawa: UNESCO Canadian Commission.

A University Degree: A Second Chance at 21 Plus. 1977. Manchester: Joint Matriculation Board.

University of Alberta. 1974. *On the Future of the Extension Function*. Report of the Senate Task Force. Edmonton. Mimeographed.

———. 1976. *The University and Service to the Public*. Second report of the Senate Task Force on the future of the extension function of the University of Alberta. Edmonton.

———. 1977. *Board-AASUA Agreement — Faculty*. Edmonton.

———. 1983. "Report of the Task Force on Mature Students." *The Senate*. Edmonton: The University of Alberta, June.

University of British Columbia. 1981. "Looking Beyond." Vancouver: The University of British Columbia, January.

University of Manitoba. 1975. "Report on Continuing Education at the University of Manitoba." Prepared by the Senate Committee on Extension Services, J. C. Gilson, Chairman. Winnipeg. Mimeographed.

University of Saskatchewan. 1973. *Extension Review*. Saskatoon.

University of Toronto. 1970. *Report of the Presidential Advisory Committee on Extension*. Toronto.

University of Victoria. 1972. "The Scholarly Community." Submission to the Commission on Academic Development by the Division of Continuing Education. Victoria, B.C. Mimeographed.

University of Western Ontario. 1976. "Report of the Senate Committee on University Planning." London, Ont. Mimeographed.

Van Hise, Charles R. 1915. "The University Extension Function in the Modern University." In *Proceedings of the First National University Extension Conference*. Madison, Wisconsin: University Extension Division, University of Wisconsin.

Vermilye, Dyckman, ed. 1974. *Lifelong Learners - A New Clientele for Higher Education*. Current Issues in Higher Education, American Association for Higher Education. San Francisco: Jossey-Bass.

Verner, Coolie. 1962. "The Structure of Community Adult Education." In *Community and Adult Education*, edited by Wilbur C. Hallenbeck and others. Chicago: Adult Education Association of the USA.

———. 1978. "Some Reflections on Graduate Professional Education in Adult Education." *Canadian Journal of Higher Education* 7, no. 2

Vernie, Coolie and others. 1970. *The Preparation of Adult Educators: A Selected Review of the Literature Produced in North Ameria*. Syracuse and New York: ERIC/Clearinghouse on Adult Education and Adult Education Association of the USA.

von Zur-Muehlen, Max. 1979. "Recent Developments in the Study of Higher Education." Unpublished paper.

Waniewicz, Ignacy. 1976. *Demand for Part-Time Learning in Ontario*. Toronto: Ontario Institute for Studies in Education.

Warren, Jonathan R. 1974. "Awarding Credit." In *Planning Non-traditional Programs*, K. Patricia Cross, John R. Valley and Associates. San Francisco: Jossey-Bass.

Whale, W. B. 1972. "The Adult Educator in the Learning Community." *Nova Scotia Adult Education* 9, no. 5.

———. 1976. "University Extension Units are in Danger of Winning Their Battle." *Canadian Journal of University Continuing Education* 3, no. 1.

Wiltshire, H. C. 1972. "The Concepts of Learning and Need in Adult Education." Unpublished paper. University of Nottingham.

Wirtz, Willard and the National Manpower Institute. 1975. *The Boundless Resource: A Prospectus for an Education-Work Policy*. Washington, D.C.: New Republic Book Co.

Woods, John H. 1983. Submission to The Royal Commission on the Economic Union and Development Prospects for Canada. Lethbridge. 10 November.

Zureik, Elia. 1982. "How Prepared is the Workforce for the Chip?" *The Globe and Mail*, 22 January.